CHRISTIAN HEALING

IN THE

MIDDLE AGES

AND BEYOND

FRANK C. DARLING

Published by

VISTA PUBLICATIONS
P.O. BOX 302 • BOULDER, COLORADO • 80306

Printed in the United States of America

Library of Congress Catalog Card Number: 90 - 071392

ISBN: 0-9622504-1-4

This volume is dedicated to the memory of

George A. Andrews Sr., Joan R. Andrews, Louis L. Chapin,

Clayton D. Ford, Alfred Gertsch, G. Eldridge Hamlin,

Albert G. Hinman, Dorothy S. Hooper, Garner E. Hubbell,

Iolani Ingalls, Robert C. LeClair, Edwin S. Leonard Jr.,

Floyd A. McNeil, Howard L. Mitchell

distinguished teachers in my early liberal arts education,

friends, mentors,

dedicated workers in the cause of Christian healing

Other Books by the Author

Thailand and the United States (1965)

Thailand: The Modern Kingdom (co-author — 1971)

The Westernization of Asia (1980)

Biblical Healing: Hebrew and Christian Roots (1989)

TABLE OF CONTENTS

TIME LINE AND MAPS

TIME-LINE OF CHRISTIAN HEALING AND RELATED DEVELOPMENTS IN THE MIDDLE AGES

(Information About Healing is Italicized)

300 – 400

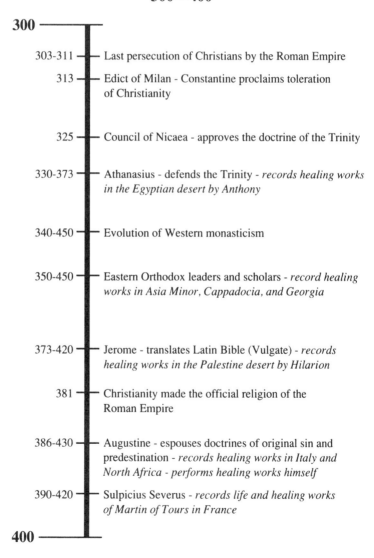

300

303-311 — Last persecution of Christians by the Roman Empire

313 — Edict of Milan - Constantine proclaims toleration of Christianity

325 — Council of Nicaea - approves the doctrine of the Trinity

330-373 — Athanasius - defends the Trinity - *records healing works in the Egyptian desert by Anthony*

340-450 — Evolution of Western monasticism

350-450 — Eastern Orthodox leaders and scholars - *record healing works in Asia Minor, Cappadocia, and Georgia*

373-420 — Jerome - translates Latin Bible (Vulgate) - *records healing works in the Palestine desert by Hilarion*

381 — Christianity made the official religion of the Roman Empire

386-430 — Augustine - espouses doctrines of original sin and predestination - *records healing works in Italy and North Africa - performs healing works himself*

390-420 — Sulpicius Severus - *records life and healing works of Martin of Tours in France*

400

400 – 600

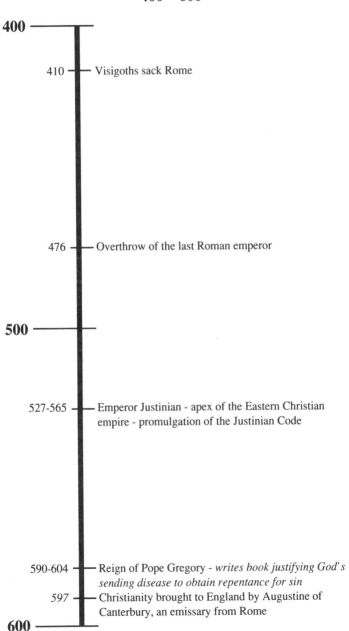

400

410 — Visigoths sack Rome

476 — Overthrow of the last Roman emperor

500

527-565 — Emperor Justinian - apex of the Eastern Christian empire - promulgation of the Justinian Code

590-604 — Reign of Pope Gregory - *writes book justifying God's sending disease to obtain repentance for sin*

597 — Christianity brought to England by Augustine of Canterbury, an emissary from Rome

600

600 – 900

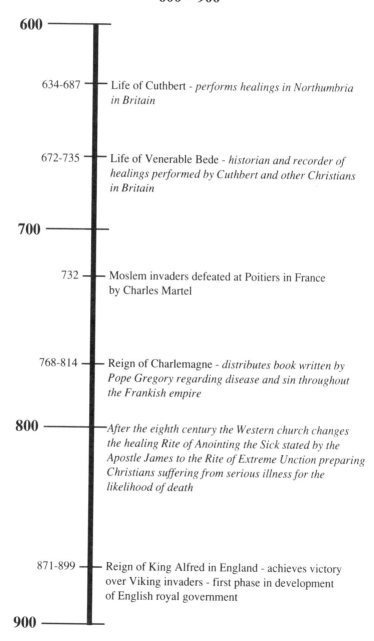

600

634-687 — Life of Cuthbert - *performs healings in Northumbria in Britain*

672-735 — Life of Venerable Bede - *historian and recorder of healings performed by Cuthbert and other Christians in Britain*

700

732 — Moslem invaders defeated at Poitiers in France by Charles Martel

768-814 — Reign of Charlemagne - *distributes book written by Pope Gregory regarding disease and sin throughout the Frankish empire*

800 *After the eighth century the Western church changes the healing Rite of Anointing the Sick stated by the Apostle James to the Rite of Extreme Unction preparing Christians suffering from serious illness for the likelihood of death*

871-899 — Reign of King Alfred in England - achieves victory over Viking invaders - first phase in development of English royal government

900

900 – 1200

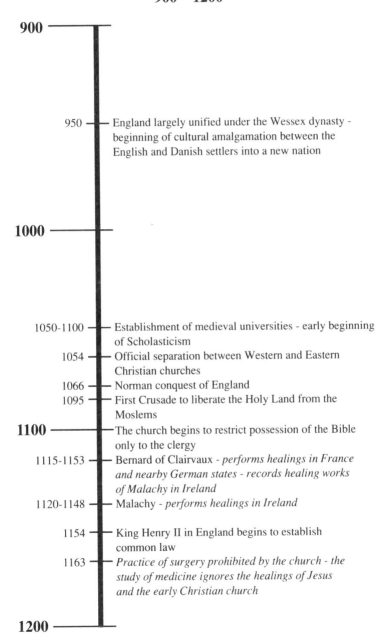

900

950 — England largely unified under the Wessex dynasty - beginning of cultural amalgamation between the English and Danish settlers into a new nation

1000

1050-1100 — Establishment of medieval universities - early beginning of Scholasticism

1054 — Official separation between Western and Eastern Christian churches

1066 — Norman conquest of England

1095 — First Crusade to liberate the Holy Land from the Moslems

1100 — The church begins to restrict possession of the Bible only to the clergy

1115-1153 — Bernard of Clairvaux - *performs healings in France and nearby German states - records healing works of Malachy in Ireland*

1120-1148 — Malachy - *performs healings in Ireland*

1154 — King Henry II in England begins to establish common law

1163 — *Practice of surgery prohibited by the church - the study of medicine ignores the healings of Jesus and the early Christian church*

1200

1200 – 1400

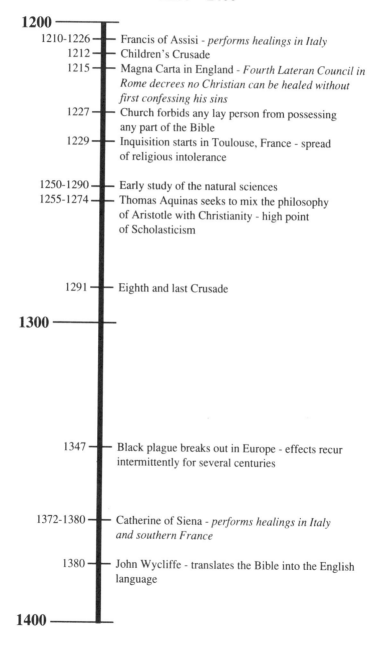

1200

1210-1226 — Francis of Assisi - *performs healings in Italy*

1212 — Children's Crusade

1215 — Magna Carta in England - *Fourth Lateran Council in Rome decrees no Christian can be healed without first confessing his sins*

1227 — Church forbids any lay person from possessing any part of the Bible

1229 — Inquisition starts in Toulouse, France - spread of religious intolerance

1250-1290 — Early study of the natural sciences

1255-1274 — Thomas Aquinas seeks to mix the philosophy of Aristotle with Christianity - high point of Scholasticism

1291 — Eighth and last Crusade

1300

1347 — Black plague breaks out in Europe - effects recur intermittently for several centuries

1372-1380 — Catherine of Siena - *performs healings in Italy and southern France*

1380 — John Wycliffe - translates the Bible into the English language

1400

1400 – 1500

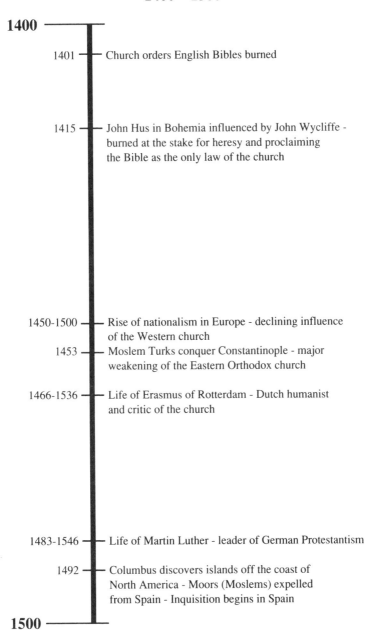

1400 ——

1401 —— Church orders English Bibles burned

1415 —— John Hus in Bohemia influenced by John Wycliffe -
burned at the stake for heresy and proclaiming
the Bible as the only law of the church

1450-1500 —— Rise of nationalism in Europe - declining influence
of the Western church

1453 —— Moslem Turks conquer Constantinople - major
weakening of the Eastern Orthodox church

1466-1536 —— Life of Erasmus of Rotterdam - Dutch humanist
and critic of the church

1483-1546 —— Life of Martin Luther - leader of German Protestantism

1492 —— Columbus discovers islands off the coast of
North America - Moors (Moslems) expelled
from Spain - Inquisition begins in Spain

1500 ——

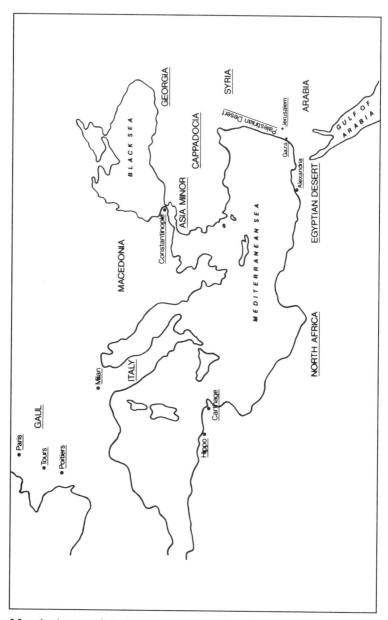

Map 1. A map of the Mediterranean region showing places of recorded Christian healing in the fourth and fifth centuries. The places of healing are underlined.

PREFACE

This book is essentially a sequel to my first study on the history of Biblical and Christian healing titled *Biblical Healing: Hebrew and Christian Roots*. At the same time, the present volume stands on its own as a coherent and comprehensive survey of the evolution of spiritual healing during a specific and important period in the development of Western civilization.

The exact time-frame of the period called "the Middle Ages" is controversial among historians, theologians, and a wide variety of scholars. The concept of this historical era is fuzzy and inconclusive. A pertinent question is placing this period in the "middle" of what?

Some scholars view the Middle Ages as the interval between the so-called "fall" of the Roman Empire in 476 and the beginning of the Renaissance around 1400. Others say the Middle Ages did not start until the reign of Charlemagne (768 – 814) and lasted until the beginning of the Protestant Reformation around 1500. Many historians sub-divide the Middle Ages into three phases: (1) the Early Middle Ages from around 500 to 1000, (2) the High Middle Ages from about 1000 to 1300, and (3) the Late Middle Ages from 1300 to 1500.

The Early Middle Ages is frequently labeled "the Dark Ages" because of its contrast with the previous classical period which brought much learning and enlightenment to Western culture. The High Middle Ages was a period when the medieval church exerted its strongest influence on the values and institutions of Western society. The Late Middle Ages witnessed a gradual decline in the power of the church.

This method of analysis presents significant problems to the student of the history of Christian healing. The early Christian church began to turn away from the practice of spiritual healing during the fourth century, when Christianity emerged as the official religion of the Roman Empire. The rapid change from a persecuted religion to the only legitimate religion in this vast and diversified region during the relatively short duration of approximately eighty years aided in orienting the church toward more secular and worldly goals.

Yet as this study will show, individual Christians continued to heal all kinds of diseases as practiced by Jesus and his disciples. This tradition persevered for many centuries after the time of primitive Christianity. Church doctrine no longer embraced spiritual healing, but some Christians persisted in performing impressive healing works. For a variety of reasons most of the recorded healings from 325 to 1500 occurred during the period of the Dark Ages. There is less evidence of spiritual healing after 1000, when the church began to acquire its greatest influence—an influence that continued for about three hundred years. Only modest healing was done by individual Christians from around 1300 until a time more favorable to the restoration of Christian healing after Martin Luther.

In the context of Christian healing this book will consequently consider "the Middle Ages" as the broad time-span from the fourth century until the Protestant Reformation. Major changes in the cultural and spiritual environments at the beginning and end of this era markedly affected the decline and revival of Christian healing.

The literature on Christian healing during the Middle Ages is extensive, and only selected portions of the writings of major Christian leaders are included in this survey. In considerable degree this work is an agenda for future research into a deeper and more thorough study of the many complex forces which have shaped the development of spiritual healing based on the Bible.

The chapters on individual healing in Part Two consist largely of original sources from the writings of these religious thinkers. Except for Part One and Part Three, I have kept my own historical commentary to a minimum.

I express my appreciation for the use of research materials and facilities in the School of Theology at Boston University, the Iliff School of Theology at the University of Denver, and The Foundation for Biblical Research at Charlestown, New Hampshire.

I am grateful to Louis Garinger, Heather Darling Shotwell, and Jane Fitz-Randolph for their assistance as readers and their recommendations for improvements in the original manuscript. As always, I am deeply grateful for the help of my wife, Ann, for her counsel in enhancing the grammar, clarity, and focus in my writing. I also appreciate the assistance of Diane Darling and Beth Darling in assisting the distribution of this book.

I assume full responsibility for the selection of the original writings on Christian healing included in this study and for my historical commentary.

FRANK C. DARLING
Boulder, Colorado
December 1990

PART ONE

MAJOR FACTORS AFTER THE

FOURTH CENTURY CAUSING

A DECLINE OF CHRISTIAN HEALING

They that are after the flesh

do mind the things of the flesh;

but they that are after the Spirit

the things of the Spirit.

Paul

PART ONE

By the fourth century A.D., spiritual healing had been a part of the Judeo-Christian heritage for approximately 1500 years. The practice of healing through the use of prayer and an understanding of Biblical teachings regarding the nature of God and man was depicted in the early records of the Old Testament. Spiritual healing never became a major part of the theology of the Old Testament, whose authors believed that God may inflict disease on man as punishment for sin. Healing, however, was included in the Old Testament as an intermittent and secondary strand of Hebrew thought which upheld God as a loving and caring Creator. This concept was that of a God whose power was capable of restoring health and wholeness to mankind.

One of the first recorded healings in the Bible was the restoration of Moses' hand from leprosy.[1] This incident at the burning bush on Mount Sinai also revealed a close relationship between spiritual healing and man's quest for freedom and dignity. Moses' healing came while he was being told by God to lead the people of Israel out of slavery in Egypt. The healing was a "latter sign" or convincing proof of God's wisdom and power that would guide the Hebrew leader in delivering his people from the bondage of Pharaoh. On the long trek across the wilderness, Moses healed his sister Miriam of leprosy; he likewise healed many of his people from serpent bites, and he stopped a deadly plague.

Another demonstration of God's power was also made by Elijah in raising the young son of a widow in Zarephath from death.[2] Shortly thereafter Elisha revived the young son of a Shunnamite woman from death, and he healed Naaman, a Syrian military commander, of leprosy.[3] These two works or "signs" were the first healings of children recorded in the Bible. The healing of Naaman was the first healing of a gentile; it illustrated that spiritual healing was available to people of all races and nations.

The legendary epic contained in the book of Job comprises a strong protest against the orthodox Hebrew belief that God may impose severe hardships and a debilitating disease on a good man as punishment for sins he insisted he did not commit. This entire allegory was probably written by different authors over a period of several centuries. It is the voice of an early "radical" and "free-thinker" advocating both divine and human rights for each individual man, woman, and child. It comprises an early petition against any form of oppression over the life of man. According to Marchette Chute:

> The vitality and power of the *Book of Job* have their origin in the fact that its hero possessed neither meekness nor patience nor resignation. He refused to accept the idea that his suffering was a penalty visited upon him by God to lead him to repentance. He rejected the consolations of orthodoxy offered him by his three friends. . .It is primarily this quality of intellectual freedom that makes the *Book of Job* so important.[4]

The story of Job reinforces the quiet yet pervasive theme in parts of the Old Testament defining God as a compassionate Maker of the universe whose all-embracing authority can restore man's health and well-being. The translation in the King James version of the Bible contains perhaps the clearest account of Job's healing and freedom at the end of his lengthy ordeal. It states: "And the Lord turned the captivity of Job, when he prayed for his friends."[5]

Much of the message in the Old Testament relevant to spiritual healing does not refer to specific incidents of personal healing. These affirmations of God's healing power extend from Genesis to Malachi. They tell of healing achieved by a recognition of the nature of God and man. They were written for the enlightenment of each individual man and woman, rather than for any particular group, race, or nation. They comprise what might be called the "promise" of healing in the Old Testament.

One of the most important promises of man's right to health and well-being is the well-known citation in the account of Creation recorded in the first chapter of Genesis: "And God said, Let us make man in our image, after our likeness."[6] Some Old Testament passages relate healing to the inherent authority in God's law: "My son, forget not my law; but let thine heart keep my commandments; For length of days, and long life, and peace, shall they add to thee. . . . Be not wise in thine own eyes: fear the Lord, and depart from evil. It shall be health to thy navel, and marrow to thy bones".[7]

The book of Isaiah speaks often of God as a "comforter." One of its most poignant references declares: "The redeemed of the Lord shall return, and come with singing unto Zion; and everlasting joy shall be upon their head: they shall obtain gladness and joy; and sorrow and mourning shall flee away. I, even I, am he that comforteth you."[8] This same book contains the prophecy of the coming of Jesus, who will bring a new covenant, healing, and freedom to the entire world. It affirms:

> The Spirit of the Lord God is upon me; because the Lord hath anointed me to preach good tidings unto the meek; he hath sent me to bind up the brokenhearted, to proclaim liberty to the captives, and the opening of the prison to them that are bound; to proclaim the acceptable year of the Lord, and the day of vengeance of our God; to comfort all that mourn.[9]

The mission of the founder of Christianity is perhaps most accurately and succinctly described in Matthew: "And Jesus went about all Galilee, teaching in their synagogues, and preaching the gospel of the kingdom, and healing all manner of sickness and all manner of disease among the people."[10] There was considerable overlapping in the first two methods of disseminating his new religious doctrine. The difference between his role as a teacher and as a preacher very likely involved the type and size of Jesus' audiences. Teaching was conducted by talking directly to individuals and small groups. Preaching occurred in his explanations to sizable audiences as when he delivered the Sermon on the Mount and spoke to large crowds on the shore of the Galilean Sea.

Healing was something totally different. In three brief years, Jesus performed more healings than the patriarchs and prophets accomplished during many preceding centuries. The early Hebrew leaders were often great preachers and great teachers, yet Jesus was the first religious leader in history to make the healing of physical and mental diseases a distinct and integral part of his doctrine.

The New Testament records a total of forty specific healings performed by Jesus on a large number of people in the relatively small geographic area where he lived and traveled. Among the 3779 verses in the four Gospels, some 727 verses, or approximately twenty percent of the total, relate directly to Jesus' healing ministry.[11] He healed both organic and functional diseases including leprosy, blindness, deafness, dumbness, lameness, paralysis, fevers, and hemorrhaging. He exorcised demons that appeared in the form of insanity and lunacy. On three occasions he raised dead persons to life and health. His most significant healing was his own resurrection from death and the tomb.

An important purpose of Jesus' healing was to restore health to his fellow man and to show his unsurpassed love for humanity. He also performed his healing works to prove the validity of his teachings regarding the spiritual relationship between God and man. In the Sermon on the Mount, he affirmed: "Be ye therefore perfect, even as your Father which is in heaven is perfect."[12] To Jesus, this truth was the basis of a divine law capable of destroying all illnesses of the flesh. In his view healing provided necessary proof in order to pursue the higher goal of Christianity, which is to destroy sin and achieve the spiritual regeneration of the world.

Healing was also a significant demonstration of Christian doctrine proclaiming a higher form of man's freedom and dignity. Jesus said: "Ye shall know the truth, and the truth shall make you free."[13] Although many people touched by his mission lived under oppressive laws that restricted their religious, political, and social freedom, they were able to obtain another kind of freedom from sin, disease, and death. These physical and mental healings were likely achieved by a higher spiritual law that provided a model of freedom to all Christians.

Jesus' commission to heal was carried out by eleven of his first disciples (called apostles after the resurrection) and several new leaders in the early Christian church (Matthias, Barnabas, and James). Paul, who also performed healing works, declared himself an apostle in spite of the fact that he never had direct personal contact with Jesus. He claimed that his apostleship had its origin in his encounter with the voice of Jesus during his conversion to Christianity on the road to Damascus.

The four Gospels and the book of Acts describe seventeen specific healings done by the apostles. Most of these occurred among "multitudes" of people. They included healings of the same diseases that Jesus had healed such as blindness, lameness, palsy, and insanity. On one occasion Peter restored the life of a dead woman living at Joppa.[14] Seven of the apostles' healings were performed by Paul, including the revival of a young man apparently killed in a fall from a high loft. The last healings recorded in the Bible were at Malta while Paul was on his way to Rome. He healed himself of a bite by a poisonous viper and restored the father of Publius, an inhabitant on this island, from a fever. Paul also healed other islanders of serious diseases. These healings illustrated that the impersonal teachings of Jesus about the spiritual nature of God and man, rather than adulation of his human personality, provided the restorative power in Christian healing. All of the apostles incorporated the practice of spiritual healing into the mission of the early church.

From the end of the period covered in the New Testament (around 100) until the fourth century, the church continued to practice spiritual healing as taught and demonstrated by Jesus and the apostles. This Christian heritage was recorded in the writings of some thirty church fathers, including Justin Martyr, Irenaeas, Tertullian, Origen, Cyprian, Arnobius, and Lactantius. This group of leaders included both Greek and Latin Christians. They wrote some of the major theological works of the early church. Many were born as pagans and became converts to Christianity. Some served as bishops of the church. Most were martyred by the Roman authorities.

The writings of these early church leaders also contain much information about Christian healing from the time of the New Testament until Constantine. The bulk of their treatises consists of lengthy apologies or defenses of Christianity directed against theological attacks from a variety of pagan and heretical opponents. Only a small portion of these writings is about healing. Much of their exposition was intended to illustrate the validity of Jesus' teachings. One of their major accomplishments was to resist efforts to combine early Christian doctrine with Greek philosophy, a goal that was strengthened by the inability of Greek thought to heal disease.

One of the most outspoken affirmations of Christianity and its healing power was written by Arnobius (circa 245 – 305) who cited several healings performed by Jesus that are not recorded in the New Testament. In his treatise titled *Against the Heathen*, he wrote:

> And since you [pagan opponents] compare Christ and the other deities as to the blessings of health bestowed, how many thousands of infirm persons do you wish to be shown to you by us; how many persons affected with wasting diseases, whom no appliances whatever restored, although they went as suppliants through all the temples, although they prostrated themselves before the gods, and swept the very thresholds with their lips -- though, as long as life remained, they wearied with prayers, and importuned with most piteous vows Aesculapius, himself the health-giver, as they call him?[15]

> By a word He [Jesus] assuaged the racking pains of the aching members; and by a word they checked the writhings of maddening sufferings. By one command He drove demons from the body, and restored their senses to the lifeless; . . .

> He ordered the dropsical and swollen flesh to recover its natural dryness; and His servants in the same man-

> ner stayed the wandering waters, and ordered them to glide through their own channels, avoiding injury to the frame. Sores of immense size, refusing to admit of healing, He restrained from further feeding on the flesh, by the interposition of one word; and they in like manner, by restricting ravages, compelled the obstinate and merciless cancer to confine itself to a scar.

> To the lame He gave the power of walking, to the dark eyes sight, the dead He recalled to life; and not less surely did they, too, relax the tightened nerves, fill the eyes with light already lost, and order the dead to return from the tombs, reversing the ceremonies of the funeral rites.[17]

The healings recorded in the Old Testament and during the time of primitive Christianity supported the development of a unique tradition in Western civilization of protesting against all forms of oppressive authority. From early Hebrew history these protests have been directed at the tyranny imposed by religious dogma, political suppression, economic injustice, and social intolerance. They have likewise been directed at the tyranny imposed by fear and ignorance in the human mind, that is often the source of disease and suffering.

One of the most vivid illustrations of this early custom of protesting against political or mental subjugation was the charge of the three Hebrew men, Shadrach, Meshach, and Abednego, directed against the Babylonian king, Nebuchadnezzar, when they refused to worship his golden image. Shortly thereafter they walked away unharmed from the midst of a fiery furnace. When confronting the king, the three captives declared:

> O Nebuchadnezzar, we are not careful to answer thee in this matter. If it be so, our God whom we serve is able to deliver us from the burning fiery furnace, and he will deliver us out of thine hand, O king. But if not, be it known unto thee, O king, that we will not serve thy gods, nor worship the golden image which thou hast set up.[18]

Jesus protested frequently against the repression imposed by the rigidity of Jewish legalism and its lack of concern for human suffering. On one occasion he encountered the bitter scorn of the ruler of a synagogue after healing a woman on the sabbath day who had suffered from arthritis for eighteen years. He declared:

> Thou hypocrite, doth not each one of you on the sab-
> bath loose his ox or his ass from the stall, and lead him
> away to watering? And ought not this woman, being a
> daughter of Abraham, whom Satan hath bound, lo,
> these eighteen years, be loosed from this bond on the
> sabbath day? And when he had said these things, all his
> adversaries were ashamed: and all the people rejoiced
> for all the glorious things that were done by him.[19]

Similarly, Tertullian in North Africa denounced the abuse of the rights
of Christians by local Roman officials during the third century. At one
time he combined his appeal for religious freedom with specific accounts
of healings performed by Christians among high-ranking Roman rulers,
including a healing of Severus, the father of the emperor Antonine. In a
brief work titled *To Scapula*, Tertullian wrote:

> We who are without fear are not seeking to frighten
> you, but we would save all men if possible by warning
> them not to fight with God. You may perform the du-
> ties of your charge, and yet remember the claims of hu-
> manity; if on no other ground than that you are liable to
> punishment yourself. . . .

> All this might be officially brought under your notice,
> and by the very advocates, who are themselves also un-
> der obligations to us, although in court they give their
> voice as it suits them. The clerk of one of them who
> was liable to be thrown upon the ground by an evil
> spirit, was set free from his affliction; as was the rela-
> tive of another, and the little boy of a third. How many
> men of rank (to say nothing of common people) have
> been delivered from devils, and healed of diseases!
> Even Severus himself, the father of Antonine, was gra-
> ciously mindful of the Christians; for he sought out the
> Christian Proculus, surnamed Torpacion, the steward
> of Euhodias, and in gratitude for his having once cured
> him by anointing, he kept him in his palace till the day
> of his death.[20]

The tradition of protest in Judeo-Christian culture, supported by a long
record of spiritual healing, aided the development of basic values in Western civilization. In effect, Biblical healing provided vivid proof of the
simple yet profound doctrine that God is good and omnipotent, that He

has made man in His own image and likeness, that He is a loving and caring God who has created man for a life of health and wholeness, and that He has the power to destroy any form of sickness and disease.

This teaching reinforced the concept of monotheism and provided a spiritual dimension to the dignity of man. Spiritual healing strengthened the idea of a divine law governing the lives and affairs of men. It nourished individual freedom and human rights by claiming physical wholeness as a fundamental right of man, and healing as one of the highest forms of freedom. Since disease may afflict people of any race, sex, class, or nation, the healing of disease available to all persons regardless of these human differences was a strong influence on the concept of individual equality. Obedience to God's law and the purification of thought required in spiritual healing were instrumental in the formation of the Western idea of progress. Abba Eban has defined the early Jewish concept of progress as follows:

> Progress in history is a uniquely Jewish idea. It might be called the greatest contribution of the Jewish mind to other civilizations. . . . The Hebrew messianic idea . . . is alive with a sense of hope and purpose. It is worthwhile to strive for human perfection, for social progress, for compassion, for justice, for freedom, for protection of the poor, for universal peace.[21]

Perhaps no greater words urging men and women to elevate their lives have been spoken than in the brief promise of Jesus: "He that believeth on me, the works that I do shall he do also; and greater works than these shall he do, because I go unto my Father."[22]

Yet the practice of spiritual healing and the tradition of protest based on these fundamental values of man began to recede from the mainstream of Western civilization after the fourth century. Jesus had prophesied this trend in human history when he warned that he must do the works of God "while it is day: the night cometh, when no man can work." [23] In a similar vein, Paul wrote: "Beware lest any spoil you through philosophy and vain deceit, after the tradition of men, after the rudiments of the world, and not after Christ." [24] The early Christian church that had continued the healing works of Jesus was gradually transformed into the medieval church that embraced new doctrines and new religious practices. This historical development significantly altered Christian behavior and weakened the practice of healing.

MAJOR FACTORS AFTER THE FOURTH CENTURY
CAUSING A DECLINE OF HEALING IN THE
CHRISTIAN CHURCH

The transformation from primitive Christianity to medieval Christianity was lengthy and complex. Many books explaining the changes of this period place the blame for the decline in spiritual healing on worldliness and corruption within the medieval church.

There is considerable truth in this assessment, but it is much too simple. While many of the changes made by the new church were detrimental to Christian healing, some changes aided in preserving certain practices which in time assisted in the revival of spiritual healing. An example of this was the custom of the medieval church to require evidence of numerous miracles by persons of pious devotion and outstanding moral character in order to achieve the high status of sainthood. The miracles consisted usually of healings of blindness, deafness, lameness, and other physical maladies as done by Jesus and the apostles. In some cases they involved raising people from death.

These healing works tended to be considered by some people as supernatural achievements rather than the natural operation of God's law. The individual Christians who performed them worked largely outside the orthodox teachings and practices of the church. Some scholars have called the Christian healing from the fourth century to the Protestant Reformation "the tradition of the saints."

These church leaders helped to prevent the practice of healing from undergoing a total demise during a long and challenging period in the history of Western Europe. Reverend Mark Pearson wrote:

> "Healing [in the church] did die down, but it did not die out, . . . As church history illustrates, whenever vital faith flowered, healing — and indeed all kinds of divine blessings — became more in evidence." [25]

Healing likewise continued in the Eastern Orthodox church, where it has remained an integral element in the theology and worship of this widespread Christian denomination up to the present time.[26] Yet the influence of the Eastern church on Christian theology and Christian healing in Western culture has been limited by its relatively isolated geographical location and its traditional subordination to the authority of the state.

It is also important to note that while many changes which oriented the medieval church away from spiritual healing were caused by its own de-

cisions and policies, some changes were due to influences external to the
church and beyond its control. These forces caused the medieval church
to speak with different voices at different times during this important era.
The church did not always adhere to a single theological doctrine. Just as
Hebrew teachings in the Old Testament were dominated usually by a
rather harsh and punitive concept of God, they also contained a second
strand of religious thought that emphasized a benevolent and loving God
capable of healing sickness and sin.

Three major factors were involved in a decline of Christian healing
during the Middle Ages in Western Europe: (1) the secularization of medieval Christian thought and practices, (2) the mixture of pagan, Jewish,
and Christian doctrines, and (3) the obstruction by the medieval Christian
church of public access to the Bible. These factors overlapped in considerable degree. They were not totally isolated and separate influences ad-
versely shaping the environment that affected spiritual healing. Yet each
factor played a fairly distinct role in causing a retrogression in Christian
healing.

I. The Secularization of Medieval
Christian Thought and Practices

This development is the most familiar to students of the history of the
Christian church. It is the most all-embracing factor, and it overlaps extensively with the development of other influences shaping medieval
Christian doctrine and practices, including spiritual healing. It is also the
most complex factor, and it includes many elements and parts.

The Centralization of Christendom Under
the Authority of the Roman Church

The power struggle to unify the medieval church under a single author-
ity was a significant force in secularizing its organization and policies.
The Christian church had been fairly well unified during the time of early
Christianity. Paul found some divisions among Jewish and gentile Christians in his missionary travels into Asia Minor, Galatia, Macedonia, and
Greece; yet he preserved considerable unity in the church by his written
epistles and personal contacts throughout this large and diverse region.[27]
The unity of the primitive church was further enhanced by the intermit-
tent persecution waged against Christians by the authorities of the Roman
Empire. In their own brutal manner, the Romans proved the validity of the
historical adage that the way to unify and strengthen a religion is to try to

suppress it. The Roman policy of launching persecutions against the church by first arresting and punishing its bishops, presbyters, deacons, and other officers served to form a strong bond between the leadership and the laity. For almost three centuries the threatened church had fostered a tradition of strong leaders and loyal followers.

The task of developing a centralized authority for the early medieval church became much more challenging after Christianity was proclaimed the official religion of the Roman Empire in 381. The power of Roman secular rulers continued to decline. The church began to extend its religious (and secular) jurisdiction into a power vacuum, and it soon asserted the role of the "major custodian of Western culture." [28]

This was an enormous undertaking done in much haste. It was also a highly secular undertaking since the empire was a highly secular organization of military, political, legal, and administrative authority. To preserve the remnants of this far-flung empire, much of its structure and policies were reinstitutionalized in the medieval church. The church likewise absorbed some of the theology and rituals of its imperial predecessor.

As the church assumed a major responsibility for law and order after the fourth century, the new "Christian empire" stretched from England to the Arabian Desert and from Spain to Armenia. This vast territory contained a large and diversified population, much of it still pagan. It also contained rapidly growing Christian communities with varying degrees of adherence to the doctrines taught by Jesus.

This condition induced a strong tendency to consolidate the primary center of Christian authority in Rome. Rome had been the capital of the defunct Roman Empire; its successors assumed that the center of the new system of law and order in Western Europe should emanate from the same city. Jesus had proclaimed Peter as the "rock" upon which his church should be built, and both Peter and Paul had reportedly been martyred in Rome. Christian teachings, including the basic doctrine of monotheism, fostered a desire for centralized uniformity; they aided the development of a unified system of religious thought and behavior in "corpus Christianum." Rome became the heart of this expanding ecclesiastical and secular order.

Other Christian centers at Jerusalem, Alexandria, Carthage, and Antioch were soon overshadowed by the growing authority of Rome. For several centuries the Eastern church at Constantinople assumed a significant role in spreading its own form of Christianity into the pagan territories north of the Black Sea, yet its influence was weakened by its subordinate status under the secular power of the Byzantine empire. The monopoly of Roman ecclesiastical authority in the affairs of Western Europe was virtually completed after the sixth century with the rapid spread of Islam from the Arabian Desert into the former centers of Jewish and Christian influence in Palestine and Syria. Within less than two hundred years the Moslems had overrun all the Christian cities in north Africa and the eastern Mediterranean that had been competing with Rome.[29]

Rome became the "eternal city" and the hub of the "mother church" during the time of medieval Christendom. By the tenth century its religious and secular authority had expanded to northern Germany, Scandinavia, Poland, and the Ukraine. The Vatican was deeply involved in the military, political, and economic affairs of feudal and imperial rulers within the territories of the church's jurisdiction. An elaborate ecclesiastical hierarchy administered a variety of religious and worldly duties.

The Roman church also established an extensive network of financial resources. According to W. H. C. Frend, the wealth of the church from its early beginnings had been "proverbial." [30] Near the end of the Middle Ages the income of Rome was more than the total revenues of all the secular monarchies in Europe. England transferred to the papacy more than three times the revenues of the English crown.[31] The church was also a large landowner. Some Christian cathedrals and monasteries owned thousands of manors as well as entire towns and cities. By the thirteenth century it has been estimated that the church owned one-fourth of the land in Castile, one-fifth of the land in England, and a third of the land in Germany. These vast landholdings contributed to the growing tension between the church and secular states.

The unification of Christendom under the Roman church and the secularization of many of its activities greatly obscured the teachings of Jesus and his commission to his followers to heal the sick. When confronting Pilate at his trial before the crucifixion, Jesus had said: "My kingdom is not of this world." [32] In his teaching and healing ministry, the preacher from Nazareth performed many healings using simple religious truths. He expected his church to continue with this work which proved the validity of his teachings, including the need to heal sin and bring about the regeneration of mankind. Christianity, he implied, was to define and uphold the dignity of each individual man, woman, and child. This value was a vital part of the Christian contribution to the principles of freedom in Western civilization. Professor Elaine Pagels stated:

> The idea that each individual has intrinsic, God-given
> value and is of infinite worth quite apart from any so-
> cial contribution -- an idea most pagans would have re-
> jected as absurd -- persists today as the ethical basis of

western law and politics. Our secularized western idea
of democratic society owes much to that early Christian vision of a new society — a society no longer
formed by the natural bonds of family, tribe, or nation
but by the voluntary choice of its members.[33]

The Struggle Between the Church and the State

The centralization of the medieval church was closely tied to the struggle between Rome and secular rulers in Western Europe. This contest assumed a major role in European affairs for about five centuries, and it
continually pulled the church further into worldly and mundane affairs.

The rivalry had several roots in early Christianity. When questioned by
a group of Pharisees whether or not it was lawful to give tribute to Caesar,
Jesus replied: "Render therefore unto Caesar the things which are Caesar's; and unto God the things that are God's." [34] Two hundred years later
Tertullian likewise opposed open disloyalty to the Roman Empire, and he
regarded it as a necessary guardian against anarchy and chaos. Yet when
voicing the opposition of Christians to many of its institutions, he said,
"What is more foreign to us than the state." [35]

The church-state conflict was subdued during the early years of the medieval church. After a narrow military victory, Constantine sought des-
perately to bolster the empire by promoting unity among factions within
the church who were disputing the divine nature in the person of Jesus.
The beleaguered emperor summoned the Council of Nicaea in May 325
to resolve this issue, and he exercised considerable personal influence in
shaping the final text of the Creed of Nicaea. Further decline in Roman
power in 381 caused Emperor Theodosius to declare Christianity the official religion of the empire. During this tumultuous period politics superseded religion; the Christian church was heavily beholden to the policies
of imperial rule. According to Pagels, Christianity "became the religion
of the emperors." [36]

Many historians say that the real conflict between the church and the
state began with the reign of Charlemagne (768 – 814). Cooperation between religious leaders and political leaders began to decline as Charlemagne expanded his power over the largest territory in Western Europe
since the collapse of the Roman Empire. Thereafter "strong" emperors of
the "Holy Roman Empire" intermittently asserted their authority over opposing claims by church officials in Rome, who advanced the doctrine of
"papal supremacy."

Emperor Otto I (936 – 973) gained dominance over the clergy throughout his realm in Frankish and German territories, although this policy led
to a reaction known as the "Cluny Reform," which gained independence
for the church for a time from imperial jurisdiction.[37] In the eleventh century a bitter struggle developed between Pope Gregory VII and Emperor
Henry IV over the issue of investing clergy by church or state authority. A
series of military setbacks by the imperial forces combined with excom-
munications issued by the Vatican caused Henry to prostrate himself in
the snow for three days outside the papal retreat at Canossa in January
1077. One hundred years later Pope Innocent III (1198 – 1215) established what historians have called a "papal monarchy" by organizing a
bureaucracy and financial resources equal to those of any secular power
in Europe.[38] It was during this rise of church domination that Rome first
used the Inquisition in an effort to eradicate heresy. Yet this period of papal supremacy was brief. The Vatican soon confronted the rising national
monarchies in England and France, which gradually reduced the Roman
church to a more subordinate position in future contests with state authority. The medieval struggle between the church and the state introduced
important relationships into Western culture that have affected the development of Christian healing to the present time. In spite of the rivalry between religious and secular authority and the extensive role of the papacy
in the affairs of medieval societies, the church has made a significant contribution to the principle of religious freedom. It has done this by insist-
ing on an independent and autonomous role in shaping the values of a
Christian society. Religious freedom was certainly not realized or practiced during the Middle Ages, but the principle was fairly well established
that the voice of religion must be heard in managing the daily lives of
Christian people.The Western medieval church did not advocate a theo-
cratic form of government, nor did it espouse direct administrative rule by
the clergy in mundane affairs. Yet the church at times came close to this
practice, especially during the High Middle Ages.

 Instead the church recognized the legitimate and necessary authority
exerted by state rulers over secular affairs. In this complex and never-re-
solved struggle, the medieval church claimed that as the highest authority
of God on earth it had a significant role to play in the affairs of a Christian
society. It expected to be a prime maker of spiritual and moral values. At
times it wanted a superior role in this process or at least an equal role. It
vehemently resisted an inferior role.

 The early institutionalization of an adversarial relationship between the
church and the state raised key questions: What values should the church

impart to the state? Who determines whether or not these values are sacred or secular or a mixture of both? What could happen when there is
more than one Christian church promoting different religious values for a
secular society? What could happen when there are one or more non-
Christian religions advocating new policies for a secular society?

An illustration of the complexity of this emerging relationship occurred
during the Middle Ages, and it involved the development of Christian
healing. At the turn of the seventh century, Pope Gregory the Great (590 –
604) wrote a book titled *The Book of Pastoral Rule*, which served as a
guide for the clergy ministering to the sick. It also contained a justification for God imposing sickness on people to make them repent for their
sins. Disease could be more useful than health, Gregory declared, in shaping correct Christian behavior.[39]

During the final years of his life, Gregory suffered from a severe case
of gout, which he attributed to possible punishment for leaving a
monastery earlier in his clerical career. According to a church historian:

> With Gregory's point of view and practice, Western
> thinking about healing had come full circle. Sickness
> was no longer understood as the malicious work of
> demons or the Evil One to be countered in every in-
> stance. Instead it was a mark of God's correction,
> sometimes inflicted by the negative powers with divine
> approval, to bring moral renewal.[40]

This view emanating from the Vatican was reinforced at the Fourth
Lateran Council in 1215; this important meeting decreed that no Christian
could heal anyone who had not first confessed his sins.

Gregory's book contained a revival of the Old Testament doctrine stating that sickness was imposed by God to punish man for sinful acts. This
view conflicted with much of Jesus' teaching and healing mission. It rejected Jesus' reply when he was asked by his disciples whether or not a
blind man they saw by the wayside was born in this condition because of
his own sins or the sins of his parents. On this occasion Jesus answered:
"Neither hath this man sinned, nor his parents: but that the works of God
should be made manifest in him." [41]

In spite of Gregory's contradiction of the teachings in the New Testament, some secular rulers were active in disseminating this unfavorable
opinion. *The Book of Pastoral Rule* was taken to England by the first
Christian missionaries in the sixth and seventh centuries, and it was translated into the West Saxon language by order of King Alfred. Thereafter it

was distributed to every bishop in the kingdom. Charlemagne also decreed that Gregory's book be given to every bishop in his empire along with the New Testament and the Canon of the Church.

These two acts of cooperation between the medieval church and the state did much to weaken a proclivity toward Christian healing. They added to a growing popular sense of fatalism and fear. At an early date in the medieval era, they indicated a need for some separation between the institutions of the church and those of the state. This period also revealed the desirability of more than one denomination or church transmitting the teachings of the Bible into a Christian community. It showed the need for religious tolerance in gaining some kind of consensus regarding the message or voice coming from the religious sector of the society. And it indicated that this should be a voice speaking accurately about relevant teachings of the Bible, including its important message of healing.

The Crusades

One of the major ironies in the history of Western civilization was the emergence of the Crusades, which started as a religious movement allegedly "marked with the cross" to expand Christian power and influence. These massive incursions into the Middle East began in 1095 to regain control over the Holy Sepulchre in Jerusalem, which had been seized by the Moslems in the seventh century. These adventuresome and costly operations over a period of almost two centuries resulted in the formation of a much more secular and worldly life-style in Western Europe, which was increasingly beyond the influence of the church.

The precipitating cause of the first Crusade was the interruption of Christian pilgrimages to the Holy Land. This region had just been conquered by the Seljuk Turks.[42] Pope Urban II appealed to Christians throughout Europe to assist in recapturing this territory from Moslem domination and to restore it to Christian control. The Vatican issued an appeal for money and military volunteers at a time when the medieval church enjoyed much widespread loyalty.

During the next two hundred years a total of eight Crusades brought Christian armies of vastly different fighting ability to the roads and waterways leading to the Holy Land. The first Crusade emerged largely from France, and in 1099 it succeeded in capturing and holding Jerusalem for almost ninety years. This military victory involved staggering losses of life among Christians, Moslems, and Jews along the route to the Middle East.[43] In many ways it was the only really "successful" Crusade. The other Crusades met with many failures and much bloodshed as Moslem forces recaptured land temporarily held by the invading Christian armies. Popular enthusiasm for this "holy" cause gradually declined, and the last Crusade ended in 1291.

The human and physical losses in Western Europe were enormous. At times Christian leaders and military forces had fought each other enroute to the eastern Mediterranean region. This internecine warfare reduced the unity of Western Christendom and aroused a growing sense of nationalism. The Holy Roman Emperor, Frederick I Barbarossa, who led the third crusade, drowned in a river while leading his forces to Jerusalem. The fifth Crusade, organized in France in 1212 was called the "Children's Crusade." [44] It mobilized and transported 30,000 children toward the Middle East by sea and 20,000 children traveling by land. The 20,000 children traveling by land reached no farther than northern Italy; only 2000 of these young people ever returned to their homes. The 30,000 children going by a sea route were deceived by merchants at Marseilles, and many were sold into slavery or perished at sea. Only one of these children returned to his home.

The Crusades had several immediate results. They virtually destroyed the Byzantine empire and civilization, and they firmly consolidated Moslem control over the Middle East. They made it easier for Turkish forces to capture Constantinople in 1453 and to threaten Austria and other areas in Eastern Europe in the sixteenth and seventeenth centuries.The Crusades also contributed to a sense of intolerance and dogmatism in the medieval church at a time when its prestige and authority were under increasing attacks from the laity and from within its own hierarchy.

Equally important were the permanent effects of this abortive military effort. The Crusades, in effect, ended the isolation of Western Europe, and they opened the way for a new secular and modernizing era.[45] Feudalism came to an end with the decline of the landed aristocracy and the rise of a new merchant and middle class. Trade expanded throughout the Mediterranean region, and a money economy began to spread to many European cities. Urban centers such as Bologna, Paris, and London grew in size and influence. They soon became important innovators of economic, social, and cultural change. The close encounter with Islamic culture exposed Europe to the advanced learning of Arab scholars, much of it based on the classical civilization of ancient Greece. Europeans were at first jolted that another religion could produce higher levels of achievement in philosophy, science, literature, architecture, and art. Yet within a short time

Western thinkers began to absorb many aspects of Arab learning and Greek philosophy.

The Crusades also revealed the extensive distance between medieval Christianity and the healing ministry of Jesus and his disciples. A Roman Catholic historian has stated: "There is no doubt that the Church made great compromises in adapting the message of its founder to the exigencies of a feudal society. Its barbaric wars, its crude anti-Semitism, its sanguinary Inquisitions, and its chase after witches, are enough to show how far compromise can go." [46] The same assessment might be made of the abortive attempt of the Crusades to elevate the cause of Christianity.

Pilgrimages to the Holy Land had been one of the major forms of Christian devotion since the early Middle Ages. Shorter journeys within Western Europe were also made to holy places allegedly containing relics, clothing, or bones of a Christian saint. Often these pilgrimages were made by persons seeking a physical healing. They often symbolized the need of people to reach out for some contact with Christian teachings which they did not receive from their local church or clergy.

There were some precedents for touching clothing or relics to gain healing in early Christianity. Jesus once healed a woman suffering from an issue of blood who merely reached out and touched his robe.[47] The clothing of the apostles likewise had been touched by people seeking healing from numerous diseases.[48] These acts showed people reaching out beyond the physical senses to some higher source capable of destroying disease.

Yet these kinds of healing by physical contact were relatively few compared to the usual methods Jesus and his disciples employed in destroying disease. At times Jesus touched the people he healed, but his major emphasis was to raise their thought to a new understanding of God and man's spiritual selfhood. On one occasion he was traveling in Cana and healed the son of a nobleman located some distance away at Capernaum.[49] Another time he healed a centurion's servant of palsy without visiting the place where the servant was living. The centurion said he was not "worthy" that Jesus should come into his house. Jesus replied: "Go thy way; and as thou hast believed, so be it done unto thee." [50] The sick servant was quickly healed.

In Jesus' view, Christian healing required no physical movement over long or short distances to some "holy" shrine or location. Unlike other monotheistic religions such as Judaism and Islam, Jesus' teachings never directed Christian thought or practice to any specific earthly place for expressing religious devotion or obtaining a religious blessing. Jewish writings for many centuries designated some special sacredness in the territory of "the promised land" in Israel and Judah, especially at the site of

Solomon's temple in Jerusalem. Islamic teachings also have given special religious significance to holy places in Mecca, Medina, and Jerusalem.

In contrast, the teachings of early Christianity had a world-wide significance and meaning. Jesus' healing practices required no movement to any sacred place nor any physical contact between a healer and the healed. The only contact needed was a spiritual awareness of the presence and power of a loving God. In Jesus' ministry this contact was most often made by a firm command or by a quiet prayer of conviction and authority. The healing ability taught by Jesus was and is universal.

Medieval Universities

One of the significant forces shaping secularism in the latter part of the Middle Ages was the establishment of the medieval universities. These early institutions of higher education imparted several unique influences to Western culture that further weakened efforts to revive the practice of Christian healing.

The medieval universities grew out of the cathedral and monastery schools that emerged from the time of Charlemagne in the ninth century. Their basic purpose was to train the clergy in their ecclesiastical duties and to revive the classical learning of Greece and Rome. The spread of higher education was accelerated after Western exposure to Islamic civilization during the Crusades.

The University of Bologna was first established in the eleventh century with organized student and professor guilds and a formal academic and degree program. The University of Paris was founded shortly thereafter, and it became a model for other universities in northern France, England, and central Europe. Oxford and Cambridge universities were organized in England in the thirteenth century. Throughout the Middle Ages all universities in Europe were chartered, subsidized, and regulated by the church or the state.[51] By 1500 some eighty universities had been founded on the continent.

The curriculum at first consisted primarily of the study of theology, law, and medicine. A field labeled "liberal arts" was added at some institutions of higher education which consisted of courses in grammar, logic, rhetoric, arithmetic, geometry, astronomy, and music. The academic program changed dramatically after the thirteenth century with the rapidly expanding interest in Scholasticism which sought to mix Christian doctrine with Greek and Roman thought, especially the philosophy of Aristotle.[52] This important development in Christian theology and its effects on Christian healing will be discussed in a later section.

During the Middle Ages students and professors readily crossed national boundaries to attend universities in foreign lands. This widespread
interchange had a large impact in shaping a new European identity and a
continental religious orthodoxy. The new educational system placed
much emphasis on the acceptance of church doctrine and authority. It did
not encourage freedom of thought or creative research.

Yet for the first time since the end of the classical era, the medieval
universities helped to arouse a love for learning and an expectation of
higher levels of cultural achievement. The universities signaled a major
reawakening in the development of Western civilization. In some degree,
they prepared the way for the Renaissance and Reformation. Will Durant
stated: "The universities sharpened the intellect of Western man, created a
language for philosophy, made learning respectable, and ended the mental
adolescence of the triumphant barbarians." [53]

Three influences of the medieval universities further weakened the
practice of Christian healing. The first was the study of theology, labeled
by Thomas Bokenkotter as the "real queen" of the "medieval sciences." [54]
The growth of the universities from the cathedral and monastery schools
caused theological studies to consist largely of courses dealing with canon
law, the various doctrines of early church fathers, and after the thirteenth
century, the large inroads of Greek (largely Aristotelian) philosophy.
Some coverage was given to the Old and New Testaments, but a major
academic pursuit was the preservation of the traditions and dogmas of the
church. Much thought was centered on original sin, redemptive suffering,
and the salvation of man's soul.

Medieval higher education gave relatively little thought to early Christian teachings. There was little awareness of the basic ideas that enabled
early Christians to heal sickness as well as sin. Medieval Christianity had
digressed markedly from the simple teachings of its early founders. It had
also developed a highly convoluted ecclesiastical legalism, a trend that
lost much of the church's original spiritual vitality.

A second adverse influence on Christian healing was the study of
medicine. In some ways the formal study of medicine was a good sign. It
indicated a growing concern for human life and a recognition that disease
should be healed. It reduced the prevailing attitude of fatalism and
showed some return to the dignity of man embodied in the writings of the
Bible. Medical studies during the Middle Ages made some advances beyond the earlier knowledge of thinkers such as Hippocrates and Galen,
and they developed new methods of alleviating physical suffering.

Yet the study of medicine revealed several theological contradictions
that were shunted aside and never resolved. The effort to heal disease by

the use of material medicine alone conflicted with the prevailing theological belief that disease was sent by God to punish man for sinful acts.

The church never explained why it should allow God's will to be thwarted by reducing human suffering through the use of medical knowledge and practice. This inconsistency was compounded at times when the church intervened in the study of medicine on theological grounds. The Council of Tours in 1163, for example, prohibited the practice of surgery within church institutions since it caused the shedding of blood. Thereafter surgery was performed mostly by barbers, a tradition still symbolized by the red and white pole standing outside modern barber shops. For more than a century the church also forbad the dissection of human bodies to assist in the study of anatomy.[55]

One of the most significant shortcomings in the study of medicine at medieval universities was the failure to revive Jesus' method as an alternative form of healing. An opportunity to advance knowledge and learning about an important Christian heritage was sorely missed.

From the time of Moses, serious diseases had been healed entirely by the use of prayer and a recognition of man's relationship to a loving and caring God. Jesus had raised this kind of healing to unprecedented heights. There is no record that he or his disciples used medicine or surgery in healing disease. At times he healed illnesses that physicians had failed to heal. The woman healed by touching the border of his garment "had spent all her living upon physicians, neither could [she] be healed of any." [56] The method of healing described in the book of James issued no call for the medical profession. It declared:

> Is any among you afflicted? let him pray. Is any merry? let him sing psalms. Is any sick among you? let him call for the elders of the church; and let them pray over him, anointing him with oil in the name of the Lord:
>
> And the prayer of faith shall save the sick, and the Lord shall raise him up; and if he have committed sins, they shall be forgiven him.[57]

In an address to the Greeks, one of the early church fathers named Tatian (110 – 172) also spoke about healing solely through prayer. He said:

> If any one is healed by matter, through trusting in it, much more will he be healed by having recourse to the power of God. As noxious preparations are material compounds, so are curatives of the same nature. If, however, we reject the baser matter, some persons of-

> ten endeavor to heal by a union of one of these bad
> things with some other, and will make use of the bad to
> attain the good. . . Why is he who trusts in the system
> of matter not willing to trust in God? [58]

The medical faculties in universities during the Middle Ages over-looked these unencumbered guidelines in healing the sick. Christian thought had become deeply enmeshed in a narrow view of man and his right to a life of health and freedom. In spite of some advancements in learning during the late medieval period, the church revealed how far it had departed from the basic teachings of early Christianity. The emerging study of medical healing ignored Jesus' influence in the study and prac-tice of medicine. This historical omission has continued up to the present time. An eminent doctor of medicine and editor of a medical journal has written:

> It has become traditional to identify modern doctors in
> spirit with a long line of historic greats reaching back
> to the impressive Hippocrates. This notable Greek, a
> veritable pinnacle in ancient medicine, often called the
> "Father of Medicine," largely set the pattern for current
> professional attitudes and relationships. But sometimes
> it is forgotten that medicine owes it greatest debt not to
> Hippocrates, but to Jesus. It was the humble Galilean
> who more than any other figure in history bequeathed
> to the healing arts their essential meaning and spirit . . .
> [P]hysicians would do well to remind themselves that
> without His spirit, medicine degenerates into deperson-
> alized methodology, and its ethical code becomes a
> mere legal system. Jesus brings to methods and codes
> the corrective of love without which true healing is
> rarely actually possible. The spiritual "Father of Medi-
> cine" was not Hippocrates of the island of Cos, but
> Jesus of the town of Nazareth! [59]

A third influence reducing Christian healing in the medieval universi-ties was the early study of the natural sciences. One of the founders of Western science was Albertus Magnus (1193 – 1280) who broadened the study of theology into an examination of the scientific methodology of the early Greek scientists. Albertus was a member of the Dominican clerical order, and he taught at the universities in Cologne and Paris. One of his most famous students was Thomas Aquinas, a major theologian of the Middle Ages.[60]

Another medieval scientist was Roger Bacon (1214 – 1292) who taught at Oxford and aroused a wider interest in the study of mathematics, optics, alchemy, and astronomy. At the request of the Vatican, Bacon wrote an encyclopedia of the sciences of the thirteenth century. He did not make any important contributions to scientific knowledge. Instead he was a philosopher of science, stressing the importance of research, experimentation, and observation in the pursuit of scientific truth.

As in the study of medicine, the early experimentation in the natural sciences at several medieval universities held some promise for the revival of Christian healing. The scientific approach to studies in several fields such as mathematics, optics, and astronomy made it possible to gain more accurate knowledge of physical phenomena. The use of experimentation began to reduce some of the ignorance and superstition about the nature of the universe. This "new" method was the beginning of a system of thought and proof much like Jesus had illustrated in his healing works some twelve centuries before.

The early study of natural science taught that the laws of matter are laws of nature, an assumption detrimental to the revival of Christian healing. This initial speculation reinforced the opinion of the ancient Greeks that matter alone has reality. It ignored the presence of a higher law of God unseen to the physical senses. It started a small ripple on a larger pond of scientific inquiry that led eventually to a unique and aggressive form of materialism in modern Western societies.

The Black Plague

The widespread epidemic of bubonic plague that began sweeping over much of Europe in 1347 was perhaps the most destructive disease to afflict a human society in recorded world history. This pestilence started at the Italian port of Messina where flea-infected rodents had carried the disease from trading cities in the Black Sea. The plague spread quickly along major commercial routes into Spain, France, and southern Germany. By 1350 it had reached England and Scandinavia.[61] The disease subsided shortly thereafter, but outbreaks continued to occur in different parts of Europe until the seventeenth century.

The plague got its name from the black discoloration and swelling it caused on the body. In most cases these symptoms caused a quick death. Some persons became afflicted with the disease and died in their sleep. Some doctors succumbed while attempting to treat their patients. The dreaded malady caused panic and fear as the people knew of no treatment or prevention. A widespread saying was: "This is the end of the world." [62]

The loss of human life was staggering. In the span of twenty years the plague destroyed an estimated one-third of the total population of Europe, a loss numbering about 25,000,000 people. The disease attacked people of all classes, although it took its heaviest toll among the urban poor. The medieval church lost many members of the clergy. In Avignon, the seat of the "Babylonian" papacy, nine cardinals and one-fourth of the clerical staff perished. In England two successive Archbishops of Canterbury died within less than a year. One thousand English towns lost their inhabitants. Europe did not return to its pre-1347 population until the early sixteenth century.

The plague occurred just as feudal Europe was beginning to emerge into the modern era, and its psychological and social effects were devastating. Another criticism was cast at the medieval church and further damaged its declining prestige. The widespread impact of the disease reinforced the prevailing theology, which focused on original sin, redemptive suffering, and the status of the human soul after death. It intensified a sense of pessimism and fatalism. It further convinced people that the events of their lives were beyond their control. In his first volume of a history of the English-speaking people, Winston Churchill wrote: "The Church, smitten like the rest in body, was wounded grievously in spiritual power. If a God of mercy ruled the world, what sort of rule was this? Such was the challenging thought which swept upon the survivors." [63]

Many leaders and people believed the plague was caused by their own sins and vices. In 1348 the pope issued an edict stating that the plague was a "pestilence with which God is afflicting the Christian people." The Holy Roman Emperor also described the disease as "a chastisement from Heaven." [64] These official pronouncements accompanied various forms of bizarre and brutal behavior. Large processions of flagellants marched from town to town flaying their bare backs in orgies depicting repentance and suffering. Rumors spread that the Jews in many cities had poisoned the water supply and thereby fomented the plague. Many Jews were herded into wooden houses and burned to death in anti-Semitic outbreaks by Christian fanatics.

Beliefs also spread that the deadly pestilence had been caused by polluted air, earthquakes, and the alignment of certain planets. Many people wore amulets to ward off the feared disease. Death soon became a major theme of medieval art. Paintings and frescoes sought to depict its horror and imminence. Barbara Tuchman described this trend as follows:

> Usually Death was personified as a skeleton with hour-glass and scythe, in a white shroud or bare-boned, grinning at the irony of man's fate reflected in his image: that all men, from beggar to emperor, from harlot to

queen, from ragged clerk to Pope, must come to this.
No matter what their poverty or power in life, all is
vanity, equalized by death. The temporal is nothing;
what matters is the after-life of the soul.[65]

II. The Mixture of Pagan, Jewish, and Christian Doctrines

A second factor reducing the vitality of Christian healing after the
fourth century was the mixture or blending of Christian teachings with pagan and Jewish religious beliefs and customs. Some of the pagan influences came from imperial traditions surrounding the ancient centers that
shaped the early Judeo-Christian tradition. The Isis cult in Egypt, for example, influenced the tradition that identified Mary as the "Mother of
God" (Magna Mater) in early medieval theology.

This practice was facilitated by the opinion that the church had replaced the Bible as the final source of Christian doctrine. The Bible was
often quoted, but only in a context officially approved by the Vatican. The
medieval church, in effect, did something Jesus, the apostles, and the
early church leaders were not willing to do. The church after the fourth
century intermixed pagan beliefs, Greek philosophy, and medieval rationalism as valid explanations of the nature of God and His creation.

The result at times assumed somewhat strange and bizarre expressions
in the church. One historian of medieval affairs stated: "The great men of
Greece and Rome were assimilated into the Christian universe without
too much sense of strain. Virgil (on the strength of an ambiguous passage
in the *Eclogues*) was received as a prophet of Christ; Erasmus felt
tempted to pray to Socrates as to a saint; and in 1498 statues of the two
Plinys were set up on the new facade of the Cathedral at Como." [66]

The combining of Christian and non-Christian thought was an extensive and complex process which lasted for many centuries; a study of its
full historical significance is far beyond the scope of this book. Some aspects of this amalgamation of diverse religious beliefs have already been
discussed in the previous section on the secularization of the medieval
church.[67] Our primary concern in this section will be to assess the mixtures in three specific forms of religious ideas and practices that weakened
spiritual healing during the Middle Ages.

Changes in the Healing Rites of the Church

For several centuries the Western medieval church continued to use the
healing rite practiced during the time of early Christianity. This simple rit-

ual was called the Rite of Anointing the Sick, and it was based on the instructions for healing contained in the epistle written by the Apostle James.[68] The rite involved the anointing of a sick person with oil combined with the use of prayer and laying on of hands. It was performed by both the laity and elders of the church. This rite was never changed in the Eastern Orthodox church and it has continued in its early form up to the present time.

Yet the medieval church began to modify this healing rite as time passed and as Christian doctrines became more influenced by the Greek idea of a separation between man's body and his soul. It was also altered as the Roman church became more centralized and hierarchical. After the eighth century the participation of lay persons gradually declined, and by the twelfth century the rite was performed only by the clergy.[69]

In the early years of Scholasticism (1200 – 1300), influential theologians in the Dominican and Franciscan orders changed the name of this healing ritual to The Rite of Extreme Unction. These men believed that sacramental rites must have a spiritual purpose, and they did not believe that healing the physical body involved anything "spiritual." The medieval church consequently began using the healing rite only as a means to forgive sins and to purify the soul. Very soon the rite became a sacrament of dying. It was performed only when death was imminent, not when death or suffering might be avoided. In addition, the church required that the clergy receive proof that the sick person had confessed his or her sins before performing this ritual. Francis MacNutt explained:

> The sacrament of the Anointing of the Sick has, in its history, closely patterned itself on the changes in attitude toward healing. Originally, it was regarded basically as a sacrament intended for physical healing. Its model was the Epistle of St. James, which instructs the elders to gather around the sick man and pray for forgiveness of sins and for healing. Later, as the attitude toward sickness changed and it was seen more as a blessing than a curse, the purpose of the sacrament shifted until its primary effect was spiritual: to prepare a soul in danger of death for immediate entrance to glory. . . . As a result, the sight of a priest in the sickroom was often regarded by the patient as a harbinger of death." [70]

This rite continued in the Roman Catholic Church until Vatican II in 1962. At that time the name of the ritual was returned to The Rite of Anointing the Sick. This rite went into effect in February 1974.

The ritualization of this method of Christian healing by the medieval church was made possible by its use of the healing rite cited in the epistle of James. This rite achieved a very useful purpose in the process of healing, and it symbolized the love and power of Jesus' teachings embodied in the early church.

Yet Jesus had employed other methods of healing, including the use of a command directed specifically at the disease afflicting a sick person. He also used an affirmation eradicating disease given at a distance from the place of healing. Jesus' primary method was to acknowledge the spiritual freedom of the infirm or disabled person, which had the effect of healing the physical body.

At no time did Jesus perceive any separation between man's body and soul for the purpose of removing only evil and sin. In fact, Jesus' healings showed that sickness and sin were healed by the same spiritual process. When healing a man diseased with palsy, he asked a group of critics: "Whether is easier, to say, Thy sins be forgiven thee; or to say, Rise up and walk?" [71] In Jesus' view, healing was not to prepare anyone for death. Instead on four occasions he overcame death. His mission was to help people have life "more abundantly" and to begin a process of spiritual growth leading to "eternal life." [72]

The changes in the healing rite came largely from within the medieval church. They were a self-imposed barrier to spiritual healing as taught by Jesus and his disciples. They distorted an important tradition of the early Christian church, and they ignored the role of healing as proof of the validity of Jesus' teachings. The medieval theologians also overlooked Jesus' condemnation of elaborate rituals which distracted men from the simple teachings contained in the Bible. These teachings explained the true nature of God and man that in turn provided divine authority for healing disease and sin.

Jesus once denounced a group of scribes and Pharisees for their obsession with a rigid and detailed form of the law, rather than with its deeper meaning and purpose. He said: "For ye pay tithe of mint and anise and cummin, and have omitted the weightier matters of the law, judgment, mercy, and faith: these ought ye to have done, and not to leave the other undone." [73] A similar obstacle to Christian healing occurred in the medieval church. Love and faith and understanding, not more rituals and ceremonies, were needed to preserve this precious legacy formulated and fostered by Jesus.

Augustine, Original Sin, and Predestination

Augustine is one of the most colorful, complex, and controversial thinkers ever to shape Christian theology. He has been labeled by many historians as the greatest Christian writer since the Apostle Paul. In *Harper's Concise Book of Christian Faith*, he is praised as "*the* Father of the Western Church." [74] The eminent British scholar Henry Chadwick has cited him as "the first modern man." [75] Because of his restless and rather licentious youth, Augustine is described in a chapter in Robert Payne's book as "The Sensualist." [76] In considerable degree these appelations have come from Augustine's prodigious writings extending over some fifty volumes. The variety of theological and worldly topics that he covered in these works brought him both fame and bitter disputations during a long lifetime.

Augustine lived during the final phase of the disintegration of the Roman Empire and the formative stages of the Middle Ages. He was born in 354 in the Roman province of Numidia on the coast of North Africa. His father was a pagan and his mother a devout Christian. His early years were marked by a wanton promiscuity that included a lengthy period of cohabitation with a mistress and an illegitimate son. A brilliant mind led him to advanced education at Carthage, Rome, and Milan. His highly inquisitive disposition also brought him to the study of a diverse array of major thinkers of his time.

Augustine's formative thought was shaped by a mixture of ideas. He was influenced by pagan philosophers such as Plato and Cicero, the materialistic dualism of Manichaeanism, and the sermons of the eminent Christian theologian, Ambrose. His theological views were the result of extensive reading in the Old Testament. He became increasingly devoted to the teachings of Jesus and the New Testament. In 386, at the age of thirty-three, he was baptized a Christian by Ambrose.

Augustine was appointed to the office of Bishop of Hippo in his native North Africa in 397. After his conversion to Christianity, he became involved during the remainder of his life in long and acrimonious controversies with the Manichaeans. He also fought against the Donatists, who formed a schismatic Christian movement in North Africa, and with the Pelagians, who opposed his doctrine of original sin. He died in 430 as barbarian invaders were about to overrun the city of Hippo.

Augustine exerted extremely diverse influences on the teaching and practice of Christian healing. His theological writings on original sin and predestination were among the most damaging obstacles to spiritual healing proclaimed by any Christian spokesman during the entire Middle

Ages. Yet near the end of his life he markedly changed his views and became active in the healing work of the Christian church in North Africa.

The doctrine of original sin long predated the life and career of Augustine. This specific tenet regarding the "fall" of Adam had been shared for
many centuries by both Jews and Christians. According to this view, all
of Adam's lineage has been "cursed" into a life of continual sin and punishment because of the spiritual and moral weakness of their primitive
forefather.

This doctrine was qualified in both Jewish and Christian teachings by
the idea of free choice. Both the Old and New Testaments upheld the
view that man could choose to follow God's law and receive His blessings and salvation, or yield to the temptation of the serpent (evil) like
Adam and Eve and receive the consequences of adversity and suffering.

The major development in the doctrine of original sin occurred with the
life and mission of Jesus. Christian doctrine upheld his example as the solution to the problem of original sin. *The Interpreter's Dictionary of the
Bible* states:

> The one factor which makes this great difference is the
> work of Jesus Christ. He provides something which the
> saints of the OT yearned for but could never find: real
> and certain victory over sin. The doctrine of sin in the
> NT is dominated by the assurance that Christ has come
> to conquer it.[77]

This Christian principle regarding man's ability to overcome sin is defined very clearly in the book of Romans: "There is therefore now no condemnation to them which are in Christ Jesus, who walk not after the flesh,
but after the Spirit. For the law of the Spirit of life in Christ Jesus hath
made me free from the law of sin and death." [78] Thus the concept of free
choice and the example of Christ Jesus were the Christian solution to
original sin up to the time of Augustine.

Augustine made a significant modification in the previous doctrine of
original sin. He proclaimed that a debasement of human nature by an in-
exorable and uncontrollable impulse for sexual gratification has caused
mankind to suffer permanent downfall from God's grace and protection.
In effect, Augustine declared, man has little or no choice between good
and evil; man's birth resulting from the act of human procreation links
him to a life of perpetual sin and punishment. Man is firmly locked in a
form of existence that is unlikely to be altered or improved.

The doctrine of predestination is closely linked to Augustine's theory
of original sin. Adam's fall, he declared, was caused by a futile attempt to

establish independence from God and create his own form of self-govern-ment. The failure of Adam's effort in this abortive move has proved that man is incapable of governing his own affairs. The vast majority of man-kind since Adam and Eve have thereby lived in a state of individual and collective rebellion.

Augustine's solution to this confusion showed some elements of his in-debtedness to the elitist philosophy of Plato and the hierarchical structure of the Manichaean religious order. The only suitable government, de-clared the Bishop of Hippo, is achieved by God's selection of a chosen few, a small "elect," to rule over a degenerate and corrupt society. The governors are an enlightened elite of baptized Christians imposing order through a combined authority of the church and the state.

Augustine did not explain in any detail how the members of this small chosen body of secular and clerical leaders are selected by God, or how their unlimited rule will be accepted by their followers. Neither did he ex-plain how this small elect group escaped the effects of man's fall from God's grace, since its members were also biologically conceived in "orig-inal sin."

Augustine's extreme doctrine of original sin was not accepted at first by the medieval church, although his doctrine of predestination appealed to ecclesiastical leaders eager to assert their centralized authority over a diverse mass of sinful Christians. Yet many aspects of Augustine's view of original sin gradually became accepted in the thought of Western Christendom. Pagels stated:

> From the fifth century on, Augustine's pessimistic
> views of sexuality, politics, and human nature would
> become the dominant influence on western Christian-
> ity, both Catholic and Protestant, and color all western
> culture, Christian or not, ever since. Thus Adam, Eve,
> and the serpent — our ancestral story — would con-
> tinue, often in some version of its Augustinian form, to
> affect our lives to the present day.[79]

Augustine's doctrines of original sin and predestination are among the most detrimental theological influences weakening spiritual healing since the time of primitive Christianity. These two belief systems have struck a serious blow against the concepts upholding the freedom and dignity of man. They impaired the idea of progress that emerged gradually in the Old Testament and reached unprecedented levels in the teachings of Jesus.

The belief that fallen and sinful man is in a permanent state of degra-dation was more fatalistic than the belief in Karma in early Hinduism.

The man of Augustine's theology, in effect, was motivated primarily by habit and instinct. He was nearly reduced to the behavior of an animal.

After the fifth century men and women became increasingly steeped in a fatalistic attitude of guilt and shame. They were much less willing to turn to God and the Bible for inspiration and guidance. Augustine's emphasis on man as an implacable sinner made it more difficult for people to believe they had a right to a life of health and well-being. His strong influence on the medieval church turned them away from an understanding of their status as the image and likeness of God. In time the church became a major obstacle rather than a help in Christian healing.

Augustine's doctrines of original sin and predestination were bitterly attacked for many years by various critics, but they were never sufficiently counteracted. Not enough was done by opposing spokesmen to show that the Bishop of Hippo had been heavily influenced by his own adolescent problems and the highly turbulent social conditions at the end of the Roman Empire in developing his pessimistic theological views.

Not enough was done to explain to succeeding generations of Christians that Augustine's obsession with the Adam and Eve allegory had caused him to deviate markedly from more promising and hopeful teachings in the Bible. These explained the spiritual nature of man and had been verified by the healing mission of Jesus and the apostles. The bishop's proposal of a theory of predestination in which a small chosen hierarchy of clergy and princes exercises authority over Christian societies and interprets the Bible with infallibility could be contradicted by a brief citation in Paul's epistle to Titus: "For the grace of God that bringeth salvation hath appeared to all men." [80]

Instead the doctrines of original sin and predestination aided the medieval church in imposing a rigid authoritarian monopoly on the religious thought of Europe for approximately one thousand years. They oriented the papacy into an intermittent and sordid inquisition that sought to eradicate heresy from the ranks of Christendom, a quest which only temporarily silenced voices supporting the teachings of early Christianity. These two precepts also made it easier for the church to establish additional theological trappings such as the concepts of purgatory and indulgences which further reduced its spirituality and hampered the mission of Christian healing.

Thomas Aquinas and Scholasticism

A third major effort in mixing pagan and Christian thought occurred during the late Middle Ages. This process involved the blending of Christian theology and secular influences from Greek philosophy, especially the ideas of Aristotle.

This movement had many implications for Christian healing. Unlike the combinations of pagan, Jewish, and Christian beliefs made by Augustine that had cast a heavy pessimistic tone on European thought, the fusion of Aristotle and Christianity had a mixed effect on efforts to preserve the healing mission of Jesus.

Some aspects of this blending process encouraged a freshness of thought, a desire to challenge orthodox dogmas, and an endeavor to gain new knowledge through observation and reason. Yet the excessive reliance on the human mind to clarify deep questions as to the nature of God and man proved largely premature and disappointing.

The trend toward a new mixture of pagan philosophy and Christian theology came from important technological and social changes after 1100. More effective methods of agriculture reaped larger food production, and additional innovations in industry and commerce gave rise to a nascent capitalist economy. Expanding urban areas became important centers of creative thought and change. As already cited, the study of natural sciences in some medieval universities provided more objective insights into the nature of the physical universe.

Dissatisfaction with superstitions and ignorance increased. There was more concern about the nature and well-being of man. A growing demand emerged for a revival of Greek classical learning, an undertaking encouraged by additional translations of Greek writings into European languages. Bokenkotter described Western exposure to this new knowledge as "earthshaking." [81] Some writers labeled this more enlightened era as "the Renaissance of the twelfth century." [82]

The revival of Aristotle's popularity involved renewed interest in his scientific methodology and his theory of the source of knowledge. This aspect of his philosophical teachings had special significance to Christian healing. A major attraction of Aristotle was his belief that man's understanding of the natural world comes from a rational capability within the human mind and by sense perceptions in contact with the surrounding social and physical environment. According to Chesterton, the appeal of Aristotle to medieval scholars was "the appeal to Reason and the Authority of the Senses." [83]

The attraction of Aristotle was reinforced by commentaries of influential Islamic writers such as Averroes, who declared that Aristotle's philosophy was "the supreme and final truth." [84] What has been called an "invasion" and a "revolution" by Aristotle's thought soon convinced a growing number of European thinkers that the universe, in effect, was governed not by God, but by natural laws. Widespread debate began at major universities over something called "Christian Aristotelianism."

The church at first sought to resist the inroads of Aristotelian influences, but it soon decided to adapt the new emphasis on Greek teachings to Christian theology in an effort to control or absorb it. This endeavor fomented major controversies inside and outside the church. One historian stated that the development of Scholasticism in the thirteenth century was "a battleground on which, for seventy years, skeptics, materialists, pantheists, and atheists contested with the theologians of the Church for possession of the European mind." [85]

Thomas Aquinas became the dominant Christian theologian in the church's effort to blunt the worldly intellectual challenge from Aristotle and to combine his philosophy with Christian teachings. He was born in 1225 into a family in the landed nobility near Naples. He was a cousin of the Holy Roman Emperor and related by blood or marriage to many members of European royalty. Over strong opposition from his family, he joined the Dominican order in 1244 with a desire to fulfill a deep love for the church and for scholarly learning.

Thomas studied in Naples and Paris. At Cologne he worked under Albertus Magnus, the eminent Dominican theologian and scientist. When Thomas' fellow students called him "a dumb ox" because of his large size, Albertus replied: "You call him a Dumb Ox; I tell you this Dumb Ox shall bellow so loud that his bellowings will fill the world." [86]

In 1252 Thomas began teaching in Paris and in several educational centers in Italy. During an active academic career, he performed several important missions for the Vatican. Despite his brilliance and widespread reputation, he was usually shy and mild-mannered. He has been labeled the "Angelic Doctor" by many writers. Thomas died in 1274 at the age of 49 while on a mission for the papacy.

During a relatively brief lifetime, Thomas wrote some thirty books, many of them consisting of elaborate treatises. He was a clear and logical writer, one of the greatest thinkers in the medieval church. His major work was the *Summa Theologica*, which he began in 1265 and had not finished at the time of his death. This work has been praised as "the summit of Christendom's intellectual achievement." [87] It contained Thomas' extensive and erudite synthesis of Aristotelian philosophy and the teachings of the New Testament, a unique methodology called Thomism by future scholars. It comprises perhaps the deepest penetration of Greek thought into Christian doctrine and ethics. Very likely Thomas' admixture went beyond Augustine's combining of aspects of Plato's thought with the teachings of Jesus.

Thomas' highly diversified range of thought was much like the equally vast intellectual foundation established by Aristotle. It included Aquinas' commentary on logic, metaphysics, theology, ethics, psychology, and politics. The element of Thomism most relevant to Christian healing was his theory of knowledge and his explanation of man's capacity to think.

Most knowledge, Aquinas stated, including much of man's understanding of God, starts with the perceptions and experiences of the human senses. There is a range of theological views regarding the incarnation of God in Jesus, the resurrection of Jesus from death, the Last Judgment, and other Christian "mysteries of faith" that have their final interpretation in the Bible and the church. These elements of God's creation are beyond human reason and are in the realm of the "supernatural."

At times Aquinas judged religion to be superior to secular philosophy and a means of complementing reason with divine revelation. Man's rational capacity, he declared, is an independent source of knowledge that can be improved and enlightened by Christian doctrine. At other times he expressed the view that reason and the natural sciences were required to expand Christian teachings for a more accurate interpretation of man and the universe.

In seeking to protect Christianity from the onslaught of Aristotelian thought by using intellectual arguments, Aquinas in effect gave ultimate authority to human reason. The nature of man as the recipient of certain inalienable rights was not "self-evident" as Thomas Jefferson would proclaim some five hundred years later. According to a Roman Catholic historian:

> Thomas was a very great man who reconciled religion with reason, who expanded it towards experimental science, who insisted that the senses were the windows of the soul and that the reason had a divine right to feed upon facts, and that it was the business of the Faith to digest the strong meat of the toughest and most practical of the pagan philosophies.[88]

Thomas gave very little space in his writings to spiritual healing. He was essentially a dispensationalist who believed that Jesus' healings were intended only to attract non-believers to the early Christian church. These demonstrations of God's regenerative power, he stated, were more important in elevating man's soul than in healing his body. The forgiveness of sins he also believed was of greater value to the struggling Christian than the regaining of physical health and well-being.

Yet near the end of his life, Aquinas began probing into the relationship between penance and healing. He also began considering the possibility that the major connection between God and man is love and prayer, rather than human intellect and reason. At this time the leading exponent of Scholasticism may possibly have caught a deeper glimpse of God's grace and His power to heal sickness and disease.

In December 1273, only three months before his death, Thomas abruptly stopped his work on the *Summa*. He spoke briefly to his friends: "I can write no more. All that I have written seems like so much straw compared with what I have seen and what has been revealed to me."

No record exists of what was revealed to Thomas at this crucial point in his life. He wrote and spoke nothing more about his approach to Christian thought. He said nothing more about Christian doctrine or Christian healing. Reverend Morton Kelsey commented on this development in Aquinas' life as follows:

> Many writers have spoken of this experience. But we know of no one who has looked at it in relation to Aquinas' understanding of how we know and interact with God and the realm of the Spirit. . . . We suggest that once he had begun to look directly at the question of human desire and need for direct awareness of God's grace, he was given an immediate vision of the healing and love which God offers to any who truly desire the divine presence. This was bestowed, not because God wanted to save his soul, but just because Abba loves and wants to express that love. There is more communication in love than in any intellectual process. Unquestionably something of the grace, love, and healing of God spoke directly to Aquinas from within.[90]

The predominant influence of Thomas on subsequent Christian thought, however, was unaffected by this brief hiatus of wonder and doubt at the end of his life. His imprint on medieval Scholasticism has shaped Christian doctrine and practice since the thirteenth century. At the Council of Trent from 1545 to 1563 his major work, the *Summa Theologica*, was placed on the altar with the Bible and other sacred books of the church. The new Jesuit order founded by Ignatius Loyola in 1534 was required to teach Thomism as a part of its highly disciplined intellectual training. In 1879 the Vatican officially declared Thomism as the basis of Roman Catholic theology.

III. The Church as an Obstacle
to Public Access to the Bible

The role of the medieval church in preserving and disseminating the Bible has exerted diverse influences in the development of Christian healing. Many influences have weakened the mandate given by Jesus to his followers to heal sickness and disease; some influences regarding the use of the Bible have been beneficial to the growth of spiritual healing.

One of the greatest contributions of the medieval church was its role in preserving the Bible for successive generations. This achievement has aided in strengthening the basic values of Western culture. It involved the dedicated labor of numerous monks and clergy, calligraphers and craftsmen, over a period of many centuries. Their work was done in monasteries, libraries, universities, and private book collections scattered over the landscape of Western Europe.

The medieval church also was also instrumental in translating the original Hebrew and Greek texts into Latin, the language of learning and theology in Western societies for almost 1500 years. Much credit for the first translation of the Bible into a West European language goes to Jerome, who was commissioned by Pope Damasus in 382 to make a Latin text of the New Testament.

For the next eighteen years, Jerome worked on a Latin translation of the entire Bible. This work is known as the *Vulgate*, and it has been the standard version for the Roman Catholic church since the fourth century. Durant stated that from this text, "its Latin formed the language of theology and letters throughout the Middle Ages, poured Hebraic emotion and imagery into Latin molds, and gave to literature a thousand noble phrases of compact eloquence and force. The Latin world became acquainted with the Bible as never before." [91]

Jerome made some errors in his translation, including an error which has hampered the use of the Latin Bible in spiritual healing. The Latin word "salvo" was rendered to mean both "to save" and "to cure" in the final text of the *Vulgate*. This was not the meaning in the original texts. Jerome's translation was one factor that oriented the medieval church away from healing. [92] Thereafter the writings of major theologians such as Ambrose, Augustine, and Aquinas focused on New Testament healings as an indication that Christian teachings were intended only to cure sins and save souls rather than to include the healing of the human body. Francis MacNutt explained the effect of this faulty translation on the healing rite of both the medieval and modern church as follows:

> In this way, the Church's attention was turned away
> from healing itself to focus on what healing repre-
> sented symbolically. Since the *Vulgate* was the only of-
> ficial translation used for some 1,500 years its effects
> on an understanding of the Anointing of the Sick were
> considerable." [93]

Throughout the Middle Ages the church continued to reproduce the
Latin Bible with meticulous care and magnificent beauty. Yet this core
book of Western civilization was made available only to the clergy. The
medieval church diminished the practice of Christian healing by obstruct-
ing the people's access to the primary written source of inspiration and
guidance in eradicating sickness and disease.

For several centuries the early medieval church imposed relatively few
restrictions on the translation and publication of books, including the
Bible. Copies of the New Testament and individual books of the Old Testament were available within the official ecclesiastical order and among
some scholars and writers outside the church. Yet after the eleventh century when the Vatican had acquired considerable power, it stressed the
view that the church was the sole and final authority in the interpretation
of the Bible and Christian doctrine.

The church took punitive measures when this policy was challenged by
the Cathars (also called Albigenses) and the Waldenses who embraced
"heretical" forms of Christianity and who translated portions of the Bible.
These dissidents living in southern France and northern Italy were bru-
tally suppressed through the use of military action by French civil rulers
and by an Inquisition directed from Rome.[94] In 1227 a church council for-
bade any layman from owning any part of the Bible.

At this time the church yielded to pressure from leading scholars and
universities and permitted the translation of numerous writings by Greek
philosophers, including Aristotle, into the Latin language. However, the
church took vigorous action in opposing any translations of the Bible into
the vernacular. Many of these suppressive measures occurred in England.

In 1380 John Wycliffe, an Oxford scholar, completed an English translation of the Bible that quickly spread among many clergy and the laity.
Wycliffe had been assisted by Nicolas de Hereford, who was condemned
for heresy and tortured by orders from the Vatican.[95] In this controversy
church officials declared that "the jewel of the clergy has become the toy
of the laity." The replacement of Latin with an English translation was described as "the grunting of pigs and the roaring of lions." Wycliffe died in

1384 before he could be punished by the church, yet his bones were ex-
humed and burned and his ashes thrown into the Swift River by an order
from clerical authorities.[96]

Other suppressive actions were taken by the church. In 1396 every
squire in England was required to take an oath not to read or possess a
copy of the Bible translated by Wycliffe and his assistants.[97] In 1401 the
church ordered English Bibles to be burned. In 1415 a church restriction
stated: "It is forbidden under pain of cursing that no man should have or
draw any text of holy scripture into English without license of the
bishop." [98]

In the early fifteenth century a Czech scholar named John Hus was influenced by Wycliffe's translations during Bohemia's struggle for religious and national freedom. Among the writings of Hus was the "Scripture principle" proclaiming that "the only law of the church is the Bible,
above all the New Testament." [99] He was condemned by the church and
burned at the stake in 1415.

Another English scholar, William Tyndale, who lived near the end of
the Middle Ages, succeeded in translating the Bible into the English language and distributing it in England. Professor Laura Wild wrote: "He
[Tyndale] believed, like Wycliffe, that to read the Bible in one's native
tongue was the remedy for England's ills." [100] Tyndale met much opposition from church authorities in England, and in 1524 he fled to the continent. He was captured in Belgium by Vatican officials, and in 1536 he
was executed for heresy.

These early advocates of the right to translate the Bible into the vernacular helped in preparing the way for Martin Luther and the Protestant Reformation. One of Luther's major issues with Rome was the right of every
Christian to have direct access to the Bible. His sweeping reforms after
1500 moved Western Christianity and the development of Christian healing closer to the idea that the teachings in the New Testament could make
all people "kings and priests unto God. . ." [101]

As we shall see in the chapters on the healings of individual Christians
during the Middle Ages, the Bible was a key factor in preserving some
spiritual healing in the period immediately following the formation of the
early church. With the passage of time, the medieval church became a
growing source of superstition, dogma, fear, and man-made speculations
as to the nature of God and His creation. The church gradually lost the tradition of spiritual healing started by Jesus and the apostles. The Bible provided an urgently needed message to counteract this weakening trend.

The Old and New Testaments compiled in a single book made it easier
for people to understand God as a loving and all-powerful Creator who

had made man in His own image and likeness. The Bible also contained many examples of God sustaining the people of Israel and the early Christians in times of trial and oppression. Importantly, the Bible taught its readers how to pray. It instructed them to recognize God's presence, wisdom, and power. It also gave its readers the courage to oppose and conquer evil in every form, including the healing of both sin and disease.

He that believeth on me,

the works that I do shall he do also;

and greater works than these shall he do;

because I go unto my Father.

Jesus

PART TWO

WRITINGS AND WORKS

IN SPIRITUAL HEALING

BY INDIVIDUAL CHRISTIANS

CHAPTER 1

ATHANASIUS

(CIRCA 295 - 373)

Very little is known about the early life of Athanasius. He was born of Egyptian parents around 295, possibly in a small desert village in Nitria in the arid sandy region south of Alexandria. He may have had some African ancestry, as several biographers refer to the dark color of his skin.[1] His name was Greek, which was a common practice among many Egyptians of the time.

It is likely that Athanasius in his youth observed the desert monks who lived in remote regions in Egypt. One of these monks may have been Anthony, whose life and healing works attracted Athanasius and inspired his major writing on spiritual healing near the end of his life.

As a child Athanasius caught the attention of Alexander, the Bishop of Alexandria. The young boy had "baptized" other children while "playing church" on the seashore.[2] The Bishop took the lad into his own household and trained him in the teachings of the church. Athanasius was made a deacon in 318, and shortly thereafter he was ordained a priest. It was in this clerical position that he accompanied Bishop Alexander to the Council of Nicaea in 325, which had been called by Emperor Constantine in an effort to resolve the dispute between the orthodox Christians and the dissident Arians regarding the relationship between God and Jesus.

When Alexander died in 328, Athanasius was appointed to the position as Bishop of Alexandria. The new church leader was slightly more than thirty years old at the time. He remained in this high post for the rest of his life. During the next forty-five years he waged a bitter and relentless struggle against the Arians, who continued to oppose his theological views despite the official decision at the Council of Nicaea favoring early Christian orthodoxy. Athanasius was often involved in major disputes with the Roman Emperor. He was exiled five times from Alexandria. One exile involved a banishment to the city of Treves in northern

Gaul. During his lengthy service as Bishop of Alexandria, Athanasius witnessed the reigns of sixteen emperors. He died in May 373 at the age of seventy-five.

Athanasius was a small person, a condition that caused his enemies to call him a dwarf. Emperor Julian once said Athanasius was "hardly a man, only a little manikin." [3] In spite of his modest physical stature, the bishop was a sizeable and influential figure in the early formation of the medieval church. He was deeply religious and consistently uncompromising in his dealings with opponents. Throughout his life he displayed intense scorn and ridicule toward the followers of Arius. Robert Payne wrote: "As for the Arians, Athanasius hated them with too great a fury to give them their proper names. He called them dogs, lions, hares, chameleons, hydras, eels, cuttlefish, gnats and beetles, and he was always resourceful in making them appear ridiculous." [4]

The exact role of Athanasius at the Council of Nicaea is not clear. Some historians credit him as the "hero" of the group defending the orthodox view of the Trinity against Arius and his adherents. Other authors believe that Athanasius played a much lesser role as an aide to Bishop Alexander. Regardless of his position at this historical council, Athanasius thereafter took up the cause of defending the deity of Jesus Christ for the remainder of his life. Hans von Campenhausen stated:

> The struggle [against the Arians] was never to let him
> go or he to let it go. For forty-five years he continued
> to wage it with unvarying tenacity, agility, and en-
> ergy, showing versatility in his methods and formula-
> tions, relentless on the essential issues, reassured by
> no partial success, and discouraged by no failures.
> When Athanasius died, he stood on the brink of
> victory. [5]

Athanasius also put his individual imprint on early medieval Christianity in other ways. He was the only major church leader of his time to preach in the local Coptic language, rather than in Greek or Latin. As discussed in Part One, this practice became a major issue in the late Middle Ages as a growing number of Christian thinkers sought to translate the Bible into vernacular languages for the laity. Athanasius also was the first church leader to approve the twenty-seven books that later became the final compilation of the New Testament. In his *Festal Letter* in 369, he published this selected list of books written by the Apostles and other writers that eventually comprised the official version of the Christian scriptures. [6]

Athanasius also exerted an early influence in defending the jurisdiction of the church separate from the authority of the empire. During his rule as Bishop of Alexandria, he fought vehemently for the right of the church to make its own doctrine and to exercise a superior role in making decisions about spiritual and moral values among the members of a Christian society. Weltin declared:

> Athanasius, although willing to accept the emperor as legal executor of ecclesiastical decisions, objected strongly to what he considered a current attempt to relegate the Church to a branch of civil government. Whenever, he asked, did a judgment of the Church receive its validity from an emperor? What Fathers ever sought the consent of kings to their judgments? [7]

This adamant defense of a separate church authority over important aspects in the lives of Christian people often put Athanasius in major disputes with imperial rule. On one occasion, the small-sized bishop seized the bridle of the horse carrying Emperor Constantine and publicly demanded an audience so he could restate his views against the doctrines of the Arians. He was outspoken in preserving a division in the affairs of Caesar and those of God. These actions shaped the early struggle between the church and the state.

Like other early church leaders, Athanasius wrote extensively in defending his views on Christian doctrine and in denouncing his many opponents. The historical record is not always clear as to which writings were actually composed by Athanasius. Some treatises using his name were likely the works of other Christian writers that he published and distributed.

Most of the writings of Athanasius were directed against the Arians. His best known work was *Orations Against the Arians.* Other important treatises expounding his views on Christian doctrine were *Against the Greeks* and *The Incarnation of the Word.* In his book *The Incarnation,* Athanasius explained his firm conviction that Jesus Christ was God, a judgment based in part on Jesus' mission of healing the sick. In defending this view, he declared: "He [Jesus] did not come to make a display of glory; He came to heal." [8]

As with most early church fathers, Athanasius' role in the development of Christian healing was not as a doer of healings, but as a recorder of healing works done by other Christians. His single treatise on spiritual healing was the most significant work among all his writings. It was *The Life of St. Anthony (Vita Antonii)* written near the end of his life.

This biography included an account of the words and works of the famous leader of monasticism about his own healing mission and that of other Christian monks living in the Egyptian desert. As previously mentioned, Athanasius had probably visited Anthony and the desert fathers when he was a young boy. Athanasius undoubtedly derived some of his intense religious fervor from his observations of spiritual healing among these rural Christian ascetics. It is also likely that Athanasius' writing on the life and healing works of Anthony was intended to expand the influence of Christianity. According to Campenhausen:

> In his account of Anthony's life Athanasius kept to the facts, but he described monasticism in the way in which he wanted to see it spread. The little book was not written without apologetic and propagandistic intentions. Without detriment to his simple and original nature, Anthony was presented as the incarnation of the philosophical virtues which are truly to be found only in Christians and can be acquired only through the power and grace of Christ. [9]

The Life of St. Anthony had considerable influence in extending the ideal of monasticism into Western Europe where this ecclesiastical life-style became more communal in form than among the isolated monks in the Egyptian desert. In many areas monasticism fostered an intense spiritual devotion that led to Christian healing. One historian wrote:

> The *Life of Anthony* . . . was a formidable document, of incalculable effect on the future of Christianity. Generations of men who never concerned themselves with Athanasius' diatribes against the Arians came to know the Pope (sic) of Alexandria only through the *Life of Anthony*. The simplicities of Anthony cut through the complexities of dogma. In Britain, France, and Germany the deserts bordering on the Red Sea were familiar, because Anthony lived there; and for them the desert flowered, and was real, and it seemed to them that the miracles performed by Anthony were such that any man could perform them if he had faith enough, and what greater pleasure was there than "to go on your way trusting in God and making the demons look silly?" [10]

Athanasius' biography of Anthony's life and healing mission also had a significant effect on Augustine's conversion to Christianity. It very probably encouraged the Bishop of Hippo to include a lengthy description of Christian healing in his major work, *The City of God,* written almost a hundred years later.

Anthony was born around 250 into a wealthy Coptic Christian family. His life was pious and secluded until his parents died when he was a young man. He inherited a vast fortune and provided for the care of his younger sister. In keeping with Jesus' words, Anthony gave the remainder of his inheritance to the poor and began a life of solitude and prayer among the monks in the nearby desert.

After numerous trials and much spiritual growth, Anthony became the leader of Christian monasticism in Egypt. He also became the most famous teacher and healer among the desert fathers during the third and fourth centuries. Visitors came from great distances to hear his preaching and to be healed. Some followers remained with Anthony among the monks in the desert.

The first group of passages from *The Life of St. Anthony* consists of Athanasius' commentary on some of Anthony's words and teachings relevant to his healing works. In the translation used here, Anthony's name is spelled "Antony."

> ¶ So he [Anthony] spent nearly twenty years practicing the ascetic life by himself, never going out and but seldom seen by others. After this, as there were many who longed and sought to imitate his holy life and some of his friends came and forcefully broke down the door and removed it, Antony came forth as out of a shrine, as one initiated into sacred mysteries and filled with the spirit of God. It was the first time that he showed himself outside the fort to those who came to him. When they saw him, they were astonished to see that his body had kept its former appearance, that it was neither obese from want of exercise, nor emaciated from his fastings and struggles with the demons: he was the same man they had known before his retirement. . . .

> Through him the Lord cured many of those present who were afflicted with bodily ills, and freed others from impure spirits. He also gave Antony charm in speaking; and so he comforted many in sorrow, and others who were quarrelling he made friends. He exhorted all to prefer nothing in the world to the love of

Christ. And when in his discourse he exhorted them
to be mindful of the good things to come and of the
goodness shown us by God, *who spared not His own
son, but delivered Him up for us all,* he induced many
to take up the monastic life. And so now monasteries
also sprang up in the mountains and the desert was
populated with monks who left their own people and
registered themselves for citizenship in Heaven. (14)

¶ We must not boast about casting out demons, nor
give ourselves airs because of cures performed; nor
must we honor only him who casts out demons and
hold in contempt one who does not. Let a man study
closely the ascetic life of each, and then either imitate
and emulate it, or else correct it. For to work miracles
is not for us. That is reserved for the Savior. Indeed,
He said to the disciples: *Rejoice not because demons
are subject to you, but because your names are written
in Heaven.* And the fact that our names are inscribed
in Heaven is witness to our life of virtue, but as to
casting out demons, that is the gift of the Savior who
grants it. Hence, to those who were boasting not of
their virtue, but of their miracles, and saying: *Lord,
have we not cast out devils in Thy name and wrought
many miracles in Thy name?* He answered: *Amen, I
say to you, I know you not;* for the Lord knows not the
ways of the ungodly. In short, one must pray, as I have
said, for the gift of discerning spirits, that, as it is written, we may not put faith in every spirit. (38)

In a section titled "Miracles in the Desert," Athanasius relates many
physical and mental healings performed by Anthony. Some of these
healings are similar to the healings done by Jesus that required the diseased person to obey specific instructions and go to a special place.
These citations also relate healings accomplished by Anthony at a distance from the person seeking healing.

The first passage is a general statement by Athanasius regarding Anthony's advice on healing. The references thereafter tell of specific incidents of Christian healing.

¶ Such were his [Anthony's] words of advice to those
who visited him. With those who suffered he united in
sympathy and prayer; and often and in a great variety

of cases the Lord heard his prayer. But he neither boasted when he was heard, nor did he complain when not heard. He always gave thanks to the Lord, and urged the sufferers to bear up and realize that healing was not his prerogative nor indeed any man's, but God's who performs it when He will and for whom He will. The sufferers were satisfied to receive even the mere words of the old man as a cure, for they had taken the lesson not to give up, but to be long-suffering. And those who were cured learned not to thank Antony, but God alone. (56)

¶ There was, for example, a man named Fronto, hailing from Palatium. He had a dreadful disease, for he was continually biting his tongue, and his eyesight was failing. He came to the mountain and asked Antony to pray for him. The latter prayed and then said to Fronto: "Go, and you will be cured." But he was persistent and remained there for many days, while Antony kept on saying: "You cannot be healed a long as you remain here. Go, and when you arrive in Egypt, you will see the miracle worked on you." The man was convinced and left; and the moment he came in sight of Egypt, his malady was gone. He was well according to the instructions of Antony which he had learned from the Savior in prayer. (57)

¶ A girl from Busiris in Tripoli had a dreadful and very loathsome disease. . . . Moreover, her body was paralyzed and her eyes were defective. Her parents hearing of monks who were leaving to see Antony, and having faith in the Lord who healed the woman troubled with an issue of blood, they asked to go along with their daughter. They consented. The parents and their child remained at the foot of the mountain with Paphnutius, the confessor and monk. The others went up; and just as they wished to tell about the girl, he anticipated them and told them all about the sufferings of the child, and how she had made the journey with them.

Then when they asked if these people also might come in, he would not allow it, but said: "Go, and you will find her cured if she has not died. This certainly is no accomplishment of mine that she should come to a wretched man like me; no, indeed, her cure is the word of the Savior who shows His mercy in every place to those who call upon Him. In this case, too, the Lord has granted her prayer, and His love for men has revealed to me that He will cure the child's malady where she is." At all events, the miracle actually took place: when they went down, they found the parents rejoicing and the girl in sound health from then on. (58)

¶ It happened that when two of the brethren were journeying to him, the water gave out on the journey: the one died and the other was on the point of dying. He no longer had strength to go, but lay on the ground expecting to die also. Antony, sitting on the mountain, called two monks who happened to be there, and urged them to hasten, saying: "Take a jar of water and run down the road toward Egypt; for two were coming, one has just died, and the other will unless you hurry. This has just now been revealed to me as I was praying."

The monks, therefore, went and found the one lying dead and buried him. The other they revived with water and brought him to the old man. The distance was a day's journey. Now, if anyone asks why he did not speak before the other man died, his question is not justified. For the decree of death was not passed by Antony, but by God who determined it for the one and revealed the condition for the other. As for Antony, this alone was wonderful, that as he sat with sober heart on the mountain, the Lord showed him things afar off. (59)

¶ Again, the count Archelaus once met him in the Outer Mountain and asked him only to pray for Polycratia, the admirable Christ-bearing virgin of Laodicea. She was suffering severely from her stomach and side because of her excessive austerity, and her body was in an utterly weakened condition. Antony prayed, and the count made a note of the day on which the prayer was made. When he returned to Laodicea, he found the virgin well. Inquiring when and on what day she had been freed from her sickness, he produced the paper on which he had marked the time of the prayer. When he had been told, he immediately showed his notation on the paper; and all were astonished as they recognized that the Lord had cured her of her ailment at the very moment when Antony was praying and appealing to the Savior's goodness on her behalf. (61)

¶ And as for those who came to him, he frequently foretold their coming, days and sometimes a month in advance and for what reason they were coming. Some came merely to see him, others through sickness, and others suffering from demons. And all thought the exertion of the journey no trouble or loss: each returned feeling that he had been helped. While Antony had these powers of speech and vision, yet he begged that no one should admire him for this account, but rather admire the Lord, because He granted to us mere men to know him to the best of our capability. (62)

¶ On another occasion he had again come down to visit the outer cells. When he had been invited to enter a ship and pray with the monks, he alone perceived a horrible, very biting smell. The crew said that there were fish and salted meat on board and the odor was from them, but he insisted that the smell was different. While he was still speaking, a young man who had a demon and had come on board earlier was a stowaway, suddenly let out a shriek. On being censured in the name of our Lord Jesus Christ, the demon went out and the man became normal; and all knew that the stench was from the demon. (63)

¶ And another, a man of rank, came to him possessed by a demon. In this case the demon was so frightful that the possessed man was not aware that he was going to Antony. . . . The men who brought him begged Antony to pray for him. Feeling compassion for the young man, Antony prayed and kept awake with him the whole night.

> Towards dawn the youth suddenly rushed upon An-
> tony and gave him a push. His companions became
> vexed at this, but Antony said: "Do not be angry with
> the young man, for he is not responsible, but the de-
> mon in him. Being rebuked and commanded to be
> gone to waterless places, he was driven mad and he
> did this. Give thanks to the Lord, therefore, for his at-
> tacking me in this way is a sign of the demon's depar-
> ture." The moment Antony had said this, the young
> man was normal again. Restored to his senses, he rec-
> ognized where he was and embraced to the old man,
> giving thanks to God. (64)

The final passages consist of a commentary by Athanasius regarding
the vast differences between Christianity and Greek philosophy. These
references also indicate the conviction among Anthony and other early
Christians that the truths upholding the teachings of the New Testament
are readily proved by the practice of Christian healing. They reinforce
the fact that in spite of the impressive intellectual reasoning contained in
many aspects of Greek thought, these human doctrines and speculations
do not explain the nature of man and the universe on any scientific or
proven basis. They are devoid of a power beyond human reason and
knowledge. Very important, they do not heal sickness or sin. On the contrary, Christians with little or no formal academic learning were able to
heal serious physical maladies through spiritual understanding and
prayer.

The following passages portray the joy and enthusiasm among some
Christians in the early medieval period as their religion for a time continued to spread, a process assisted in many places by the practice of spiritual healing. During this turbulent period, paganism and the ideas of
many Greek philosophers were declining.

> ¶ We Christians, therefore, possess religious truth not
> on the basis of Greek philosophical reasoning, but
> founded on the power of faith vouchsafed us by God
> through Jesus Christ. And as for the truth of the ac-
> count given, note how we who have remained unlet-
> tered believe in God, recognizing from His works His
> Providence over all things. And as for our faith being
> something effectual, note how we lean upon our belief
> in Christ, while you take support from sophistical

wranglings over words; and your phantom idols are passing into desuetude, but our faith is spreading everywhere.

And you with your syllogisms and sophisms are not converting anybody from Christianity to paganism; but we, teaching faith in Christ, are stripping your gods of the fear they inspired, now that all are recognizing Christ as God and the Son of God. You with all your elegant diction do not hinder the teaching of Christ; but we by mentioning the name of the crucified Christ drive away all the demons whom you fear as gods. Where the Sign of the Cross appears, there magic is powerless and sorcery ineffectual. (78)

¶ Indeed, tell us, where are now your oracles? Where are the incantations of the Egyptians? Where are the phantom illusions of the magicians? When did all these things cease and lose their significance? Was it not when the Cross of Christ came? Wherefore, is it this that deserves scorn, and not rather the things that have been done away with by it and proved powerless? This, too, is remarkable, the fact that your religion was never persecuted; on the contrary, among men it is held in honor in every city. Christ's followers, however, are persecuted, and yet it is our cause that flourishes and prevails, not yours.

Your religion, for all the tranquility and protection it enjoys, is dying; whereas the faith and teaching of Christ, scorned by you and persecuted by the rulers, has filled the world. When was there a time that the knowledge of God shone forth so brightly? Or when was there a time that continence and the virtue of virginity so showed itself? Or when was death so despised as when the Cross of Christ came? And this no one doubts when he sees the martyrs despising death for Christ's sake, or sees the virgins of the Church who for Christ's sake keep their bodies pure and undefiled. (79)

¶ These are proofs sufficient to show that faith in Christ is the only true religion. Still, here you are - you who seek for conclusions based on reasoning, you have no faith! We, however, do not prove as our teacher said, *in persuasive words of Greek wisdom;* but it is by faith that we persuade men, faith which tangibly precedes any constructive reasoning of arguments. See here we have with us some who are suffering from demons. These were people who had come to him troubled by demons; bringing them forward, he said: "Either cleanse these by your syllogisms and by any art or magic you wish, calling on your idols; or, if you cannot, then stop fighting us and see the power of the Cross of Christ." Having said this, he invoked Christ and signed the afflicted with the Sign of the Cross, repeating the action a second and third time.

And at once the persons stood up completely cured, restored to their right mind and giving thanks to the Lord. The so-called philosophers were astonished and really amazed at the man's sagacity and at the miracle performed. But Antony said: "Why do you marvel at this? It is not we who do it, but Christ who does these things through those who believe in Him. Do you, therefore, also believe, and you will see that it is not wordcraft which we have, but faith through love that works for Christ; and if you, too, will make this your own, you will no longer seek arguments from reason, but will consider faith in Christ sufficient by itself." (80)

¶ Such is the story of Antony. We must not show ourselves skeptical when it is through a man that all these great wonders came to pass. For it is the promise of the Savior who says: *If you have faith as a grain of mustard seed, you shall say to this mountain: 'Remove hence!' and it shall remove; and nothing shall be impossible to you.* And again: *Amen, amen, I say to you, if you ask the Father anything in my name, He will give it to you. . . .Ask and you shall receive.* And it is He who said to His disciples and to all who believe in Him: *Heal the sick; . . .cast out the demons; freely you have received, freely give.* (83)

CHAPTER 2

JEROME

(CIRCA 342 – 420)

One aspect of Jerome's influence on Christian healing has already been discussed in Part One. This was the reference to his mistranslation of some important words in the Latin Bible (*The Vulgate*). Jerome's use of the Latin word "salvo" to mean both "to save" and "to cure" oriented the thought of the early medieval church away from the physical healings achieved by Jesus and the apostles, and concentrated attention on the theological endeavor to save men's souls from transgression and sin.

Jerome was born around 342 in the town of Stridon in the Latin-speaking province of Dalmatia, which is today a region in Yugoslavia. His full name was Eusebius Hieronymus Sophronius, which means "the reverend, holy-named sage." [1] Little is known about his childhood except that his parents were Christians who evidently had sufficient wealth to send their son to Rome for his education at the age of twelve. The young man became an avid student of the Roman classics, and his collection of books soon became one of the best private libraries of his time. [2]

Jerome, like Augustine, became a fun-loving and promiscuous youth for a number of years. Gradually he became interested in the teachings of Christianity. He was baptized at the age of nineteen, probably by Pope Liberius, and he became increasingly devoted to asceticism and the life of a scholar. While traveling in Gaul, he became enamoured with monasticism and began a deep study of the Bible.

Jerome traveled to the Holy Land in 373, and for several years he lived as a hermit in the desert searching for truth and tranquility. He found this habitat too isolated and too detached from the important changes taking place in the empire. He learned that he preferred a more active role as a scholar and theological spokesman. During this time Jerome learned Greek, and he became proficient in translating portions of the writings of Origen and Eusebius into Latin. He also became the first Latin Christian to learn Hebrew, and he was soon recognized as the most proficient scholar of the Bible in the early medieval church. At this time he became ordained as a priest.

In 382 Jerome went to Rome and became a personal secretary to Pope Damasus. At the pontiff's request he translated parts of the Bible and additional writings of the Greek church fathers into Latin. Involvement in bitter personal and theological disputes caused him to return to the Holy Land, where he remained until his death in 420.

Jerome settled in Bethlehem, where he established a monastery, a convent, and a hostel for pilgrims. Visitors from all parts of the empire came to him for advice and consultation about many controversies within the church. He remained attached to his monastic way of life, and he began one of the most prodigious writing careers in the history of the Christian church.

Jerome, like Athanasius, had a complex and unstable disposition that influenced his role in shaping the development of the church. He was often kind and compassionate to children, women, and the poor; yet he frequently showed a bitter intolerance and an explosive temper when dealing with his many critics. He continued to be ascetic and scholarly, and at the same time his sensuality often elicited intense anguish and repentance. Robert Payne wrote:

> And all the time the quiet scholar in his Bethlehem study concealed his own passions and his welling hysteria, his direct violence and devastating sensuality, behind the orderly rows of his own books. Sometimes the books fall down, and for a brief moment we see the tormented man jumping and quivering like a twisted nerve. . . .
>
> He hated the flesh, but he wept with uncontrollable abandon when his closest friends died. He was atrociously inhuman, and yet human. The man who squandered so much of the richness of his mind on the impeccable translation we know as the Vulgate could fume and rant about women waving their hair, or putting rouge on their lips. He said that a man who called a girl "honey" (*mel meum*) was committing sin. He had no love for common humanity, but he had great sorrow for poverty amid the splendor of Rome. . . .[3]

Jerome's positive influence on the development of Christian healing was through his own writings, rather than through his translations of the

Bible. It was much like the role of Athanasius, who composed the very useful biography of Anthony. The historical record shows no healing works performed by Jerome; his main contribution was that of a recorder of spiritual healing done by other Christians.

His primary writing on Christian healing was *The Life of Hilarion,* a beautifully and simply written account of the numerous healing works of this famous desert father. Morton Kelsey stated:

> Jerome addressed the subject of healing but it was not part of his personal experience. He nevertheless accepted the reality of such experience: his letters referred again and again to the miracles of Jesus and others as if he were seeing them as he walked with the disciples on sacred ground. But healing as a present possibility he knew mainly through the lives of others. [4]

In addition to his enormously time-consuming projects of translating the Bible and other religious writings into Latin, Jerome became deeply interested in the healing missions among the monastic monks in Egypt and the Holy Land. His writing on the life of Hilarion tells with great clarity and conviction the accomplishments of another individual Christian who followed Jesus' command to heal the sick.

The first passages from *The Life of Hilarion* portray in Jerome's own words the early life and mission of this gifted Christian thinker. They explain in colorful detail some of the background of Anthony's influence on Hilarion and the establishment of another widespread healing mission in the Egyptian and Palestinian desert during the fourth and fifth century.

> ¶ Before beginning to write the life of blessed Hilarion, I call upon the Holy Spirit dwelling within him that He who has bestowed upon him such abundant virtues may grant me the power to describe these virtues, so that my words may equal his deeds. . . .

> Now I must tell the story of the conversation and life of a man so great and so unusual that Homer himself, were he present, would envy the subject or be overcome by it. Although St. Epiphanius, Bishop of Salamis in Cyprus, who knew Hilarion intimately, has written his praise in a brief letter that is commonly read, it is nevertheless one thing to praise in generalities a man who is dead, and quite another to portray

his specific virtues. With all good will, therefore, and with no intention of disrespect toward the bishop, we undertake to carry forward the task he began. . . . (1)

¶ Hilarion was born in Tabatha, a village of southern Palestine, about five miles from Gaza. His parents were dedicated to the worship of idols and the boy grew up, as the saying goes, a rose among thorns. He was sent to Alexandria to be educated in the school of a grammarian. There, so far as his youth allowed, he gave, in short time, extraordinary proofs of talent and character; he was beloved by all and skilled in the art of oratory. Greater than all these accomplishments, however, was his belief in our Lord Jesus. The mad excitement of the circus, the bloody contests of the arena, the extravagance of the theatre did not thrill him, for his sole pleasure was in the congregation of the Church. (2)

¶ Then Hilarion heard of the celebrated Anthony, whose name was on the lips of all Egypt, and was seized with so ardent a longing to see him that he set out to find him in the wilderness. Upon meeting him, he changed his whole mode of life and remained close by him for almost two months, intently observing his way of living, the gravity of his conduct, his frequent prayer, his meekness and humility in dealing with the brothers, his severity in correcting them, his eagerness to exhort them, and finally, his stern continency and mortification in eating, which no infirmity ever interrupted.

Thereupon, Hilarion went back to his own country, taking with him a few monks. As his parents had died while he was away, he gave a part of his possessions to his brothers and the rest to the poor, reserving nothing at all for himself, because he feared either the example or the punishment of Ananias and Saphira recorded in the Acts of the Apostles. He was, moreover, especially mindful of the words of our Lord: 'Every one of you that doth not renounce all that he possesseth, cannot be My disciple.'

At that time he was only fifteen years old. Thus stripped of all his possessions, but armed in Christ, he entered the wilderness seven miles from Maiuma, the port of Gaza, in that part of the desert which curves to the left as one goes along the coast to Egypt. Although the place was stained with the blood of the victims of brigands, and friends and relatives strongly warned him of the menacing danger, he despised death in order to escape death. (3)

The second group of readings relates specific physical healings done by Hilarion. They include the healing of children, the healing of a German body-guard in Constantine's army, and a healing of a large animal. In some of these healings Jerome tells of Hilarion weeping just before he restored a diseased person to health and comfort. A similar expression was made in other incidents of spiritual healing.

On one occasion — at the raising of Lazarus from death — Jesus had also wept. This sign was certainly not an indication of weakness or helplessness in Christian healing, since a remarkable recovery immediately followed. It is possible that the act of weeping was an expression of compassion combined with a deep regret at the lack of understanding among the people present in the power of God to heal any kind of human affliction.

¶ By the time he had spent twenty-two years in the desert, he was widely known by reputation throughout the cities of Palestine. A certain woman of Eleutheropolis, finding herself despised by her husband because of her sterility — after fifteen years of married life she had brought forth no children — was the first who dared to intrude upon blessed Hilarion's solitude.

While he was still unconscious of her approach, she suddenly threw herself at his knees saying: 'Forgive my boldness, forgive my importunity. Why do you turn away your eyes? Why do you shun my pleas? Do not look upon me as a woman, but as a creature to be pitied, as one of the sex that brought forth the Redeemer, for "they that are whole need not the physician: but they that are sick."

He stood still, and, finally aware of the woman, asked her why she had come and why she was weeping.

When he learned of the cause of her grief, raising his
eyes to heaven, he commanded her to have faith and to
believe. He followed her departure with tears. When a
year had gone by, he saw her with her son. (13)

¶ This, the beginning of his miraculous works, was
followed by another and greater miracle. Aristaenete,
the wife of Elpidius, who later became praetorian prefect, a woman well known among her own people and
even more renowned among the Christians, returning
with her husband and their children from blessed Anthony, was detained at Gaza by the illness of her sons.
There, either because of the infected atmosphere or (as
it later appeared) for the glory of Hilarion, servant of
God, they were seized with a semitertian ague which
the physicians pronounced incurable. The distraught
mother was crushed with grief and ran from one to the
other of what seemed to be the corpses of her three
children, not knowing which one to mourn for first.

Then, hearing that there was a certain monk in the
desert nearby [who might help her], she laid aside her
matronly dignity and, remembering only that she was
a mother, set out [on foot] to find him, accompanied
by maid-servants and eunuchs. With difficulty, her
husband finally persuaded her to ride on an ass. When
she found Hilarion, pleading for his intercession, she
said: 'I beseech you through the most merciful Jesus
our Lord, through His Cross and His Blood, that you
restore me my three sons, that the name of the Lord
our Saviour may be glorified in the city of the Gen-
tiles, and that His servant may enter Gaza and overthrow the idol, Marmas.'

He refused, saying that he had never left his cell and
that it was not his custom to enter even a small village,
much less the city. The desperate woman prostrated
herself before him, crying out again and again: 'Hilarion, servant of Christ, give me back my children; Anthony watched over them in Egypt, you must save them
in Syria.' All who were present wept, and Hilarion himself wept, too, in pity, but he continued to refuse to go.

To make a long story short, the woman would not leave until he promised her that he would enter Gaza after sundown. In Gaza, he stopped at the bedside of each child and, gazing sorrowfully at the feverish body, he invoked Jesus. O wonderful virtue! As from three fountains, perspiration burst forth from each one. In the same hour, the children took food, recognized their moaning mother and, blessing God, they covered the hands of the saint with kisses.

When word of this miracle spread far and wide, people from Syria and Egypt flocked to him eagerly, with the result that many believed in Christ and decided to become monks. Up to that time, there had been no monasteries in Palestine nor had anyone known of any monk in Syria before Hilarion. He was the founder, inspiration, and teacher there of monastic life and service to God. Our Lord Jesus had His senior servant Anthony in Egypt and His junior, Hilarion, in Palestine. (14)

¶ Facidia is a small suburb of Rhinocorura, a city of Egypt. From this village a woman who had been blind for ten years was brought to blessed Hilarion. On being presented to him by the brothers (already there were many monks with him), she told him that she had bestowed all her substance on physicians.

To her the saint replied: 'If what you lost on physicians you had given to the poor, Jesus the true Physician would have healed you.' Whereupon she cried aloud and implored him to have mercy on her. Then, following the example of the Saviour, he rubbed spittle upon her eyes and she was immediately cured. (15)

¶ A charioteer, from Gaza also, was struck by a demon while in his chariot and his whole body so completely stiffened that he could neither move his hand nor bend his neck. He was carried on a stretcher to the saint, able to move only his tongue to indicate his petition, but he heard and understood that he could not be healed until he believed in Jesus and renounced his former occupation. He believed, he promised, he was cured, rejoicing more in the salvation of his soul than in the cure of his body. (16)

¶ Then there was the very powerful young man named Messicas from the district of Jerusalem, who was very proud of his strength. He boasted that he could carry fifteen pecks of grain for a long time and a great distance. He considered it the peak of his prowess that he could surpass the asses in endurance.

He became afflicted by the worst kind of demon, so that nothing could hold him, not chains, not fetters, nor bolted doors. He had even bitten off the noses and ears of many people; of some he had broken the legs; others he had strangled. He had, in fact, aroused such great terror in everybody that, covered with chains and pulled by ropes from all sides, he was dragged to the monastery like a raging bull. When the brothers caught sight of him, they were thoroughly frightened (for he was of towering size) and reported him at once to the father.

Right from where he was sitting, the saint ordered the poor creature to be brought to him and released. When he was set free, he said to him: 'Bow your head and come.' The youth, trembling and twisting his neck, did not dare to look at him in the face and then, all of a sudden, laying aside his ferocity, began to lick the feet of the man seated before him. Finally, the demon that had possessed the youth was wrenched out of him by exorcism on the seventh day. (17)

¶ Then, there is the story of Orion, a prominent and very wealthy citizen of the city of Haila, situated on the coast of the Red Sea. Having been possessed by a legion of devils, he was led to Hilarion. His hands, neck, sides, and feet were loaded with iron; his wild eyes were menacing with the savagery of madness. While the saint was walking along with the brothers, interpreting for them some passage from Scripture, the mad man broke away from those who were holding

him, caught up the saint from behind, and raised him
high into the air.

A cry rose up from everybody, for they feared that he
would crush that body so consumed from fasting. The
saint laughed, however, and said: 'Silence, and leave
my wrestler to me.' Reaching his hand back over his
shoulder, he seized the madman by the hair and pulled
him [over his shoulders and flung him] before his feet.
Then, spreading out both arms from his sides, he stood
upon his hands [and prevented him from moving], at
the same time repeating: 'Be tortured, you band of
demons, be tortured.' With this, the maniac howled
and arched his head against the ground. 'Lord Jesus,'
prayed the saint, 'release this miserable creature, release this captive. As You have the power to conquer
one, You have the power to conquer many.'

I shall now mention a thing unheard of: from the
mouth of one man there actually came forth many different voices, that resounded like the confused shouts
of a populace. He, too, was cured, and not long after returned to the monastery with his wife and children,
bringing ever so many gifts as if to pay his thanks. (18)

¶ Who, indeed, could pass over in silence the case of
Zananus of Maiuma? While he was hewing stones for
building purposes along the sea coast not far from the
monastery, he was stricken with a total paralysis. His
fellow laborers carried him to the saint, and immediately he was able to return to his work. (19)

¶ Hilarion's fame extended not only throughout Palestine and the neighboring cities of Egypt and Syria, but
also to the distant provinces. There was an officer in
the bodyguard of Emperor Constantine whose red hair
and fair skin indicated his origin. (His country, which
lay between the Saxons and the Alemanni, not great in
size but powerful, was referred to as Germany by the
historians, but is now called Francia.)

For a long time, that is, from his infancy, this military
officer had been possessed by a demon that caused

him to scream, groan, and gnash his teeth during the
night. He secretly petitioned the emperor for a post-
warrant, stating his reason for the request with frank
simplicity. His petition was granted and he also pro-
cured a letter to the governor of Palestine. He was,
therefore, conducted to Gaza with great honor by the
imperial escort.

When he inquired there of the municipal senators
where the monk Hilarion dwelt, the people of Gaza
became quite disturbed and, thinking that he had been
sent by the emperor, led him directly to the monastery.
They extended this courtesy both as a gesture of respect to so distinguished a person and as an act of
homage to Hilarion in satisfaction for their past of-
fenses against him.

It happened that, at the moment, the old man was
strolling along on the soft sands, murmuring to himself one of the psalms. Becoming aware of the great
throng approaching, he stopped, waited, and greeted
them all with a blessing. An hour later, he asked the
others to withdraw and the possessed man to remain
with his servants and public attendants, for, from the
look in his eyes and the expression on his face, he
knew his reason for coming.

As soon as the servant of God began to question him,
he rose in the air, suspended, with his toes scarcely
touching the ground, and, roaring loudly, answered in
Syriac, the same language in which he was being in-
terrogated. From the lips of a barbarian who knew
only Frankish and Latin came such pure Syriac that
not a sibilant, not an aspirate, not a Palestinian idiom
was lacking. He confessed by what order of events the
demon had entered him.

Then, that the interpreters who knew only Greek and
Latin might understand what was going on, Hilarion
questioned him again in Greek. The man gave the
same answers in Greek, excusing the many occasions
on which he had taken part in wizardry and the many

times that he had found it necessary to use magical arts. 'I don't care,' Hilarion said, 'how you gained entrance, but in the name of Jesus Christ, I command you to depart.'

And the demon departed. With homely simplicity, the officer offered the saint ten pounds of gold. Hilarion refused the gift and gave him a barley loaf instead, with the admonition that they who are nourished by such food look upon gold as mere clay. (22)

¶ Not only human beings, but brute animals also, foaming with rage, were brought to Hilarion daily. Among these was a Bactrian camel of enormous size which had trampled many people to death. More than thirty men, amid a great clamor, dragged the beast along by strong ropes. Its eyes were bloody, its mouth was foaming, its rolling tongue was swollen, but terrible above all were the mighty roars that it let out.

The old man ordered the animal to be released. Immediately, those who had been pulling it, as well as those who were with Hilarion, fled away in all directions. He alone stood fearless in its path and said in Syriac: 'You do not frighten me, demon, with your huge bulk of body; whether in a little fox or in a camel, you are one and the same.'

All this time he was standing with his hand stretched forth before him. The beast that had come to him, raging, as if about to devour him, suddenly crouched down and placed its head submissively to the ground. To the amazement of everyone, its savage wildness suddenly changed to tame gentleness. The old man used this opportunity to teach how the Devil even took possession of beasts of burden, for so burning, indeed, is his hatred of man that he longs not only to destroy him but also his possessions.

To illustrate this point he set before them the example of blessed Job whom the Devil was not permitted to tempt until he had destroyed all his substance. Nor ought it upset anyone, he added, that by the Lord's command two thousand swine were destroyed by demons, for those who had witnessed the miracle could not have believed that so many devils went out of one man unless a vast number of swine, driven by almost a legion, perished at the same time. (23)

¶ Hilarion remained at Paphos for a period of two years, but, always thinking about flight, he sent Hesychius to Palestine to greet the brothers and look over the ashes of his monastery, with instructions to return in the spring. When he returned, Hilarion wanted to sail back to Egypt to those places called Bucolia, where there were no Christians, but only a fierce barbarian people. Hesychius, however, persuaded him to retire to a more remote part of that same island. . . .

On one particular day, however, when he went into his garden, he found a man lying before the gate, totally paralyzed. He asked Hesychius who he was and how he came there. Hesychius explained that he was the procurator of the villa nearby, to whom the garden in which they were rightly belonged.

Hilarion wept and, stretching out his hand to the man lying before him said: 'I bid you in the name of our Lord Jesus Christ, to arise and walk.' Miraculous speed! With the words scarcely spoken, the paralytic's legs regained their vigor and the man rose firmly to his feet.

Later, when this miracle became known, the needs of a great many drove them to surmount the barriers of distance and impassability. The inhabitants of the farms in the country around were intent on one thing alone — that Hilarion in no way escape, for the rumor had been current that he could not long remain in the same place. This practice was not the result of any restlessness or childish caprice; he fled honour and the importunity of the public, desiring, only and always, silence and a humble, hidden life. (43)

At the end of his biography, Jerome concluded with a reminder of the important impact of Hilarion's healings on the spread of Christianity throughout the region of Palestine. This is the same area where many similar healings had taken place during the time of early Hebrew prophets and in the healing mission of Jesus and the apostles.

> ¶ There would not be time if I wished to tell of all the signs and wonders performed by Hilarion, for he had been raised by God to such glory that Anthony, hearing about the ascetic and holy routine of his life, wrote to him and with pleasure received letters in return. Whenever the sick and infirm came to Anthony from any part of Syria, he would say to them: 'Why did you weary yourselves with so long a journey when you have right there in Syria my son Hilarion?'

> Because of Hilarion's example, monasteries began to appear throughout all of Palestine and all the monks eagerly hastened over to him. Anthony, seeing this, praised the grace of the Lord and encouraged individuals to strive after the perfection of their souls, saying: ' "the fashion of this world passeth away" and that is the true life which is purchased by the discomfort of the present life.' (24)

CHAPTER 3

AUGUSTINE

(342 – 430)

It is very possible that the enormous complexity and diversity in Augustine's life and mind were most vividly shown in his attitude toward Christian healing. In his early years he succumbed to prolonged periods of sensualism and licentiousness. He embraced Manichaeanism with its mixtures of an elaborate mythology, a dualistic Gnostic creed upholding the coexistence of God and the devil, and the presence of three Jesuses.

After his conversion to Christianity in his early thirties, Augustine combined many elements of Jesus' teachings with Plato's philosophy. He relied on the account of creation in the second chapter of Genesis to develop a highly deterministic concept of original sin. And from a variety of sources he advocated his doctrine of predestination.

As discussed briefly in Part One, virtually all of these ideas elucidated in his voluminous writings were extremely inimical to Christian healing. Yet near the end of his life, Augustine began to reassess many of his views on Jesus' teachings, and he gradually became an articulate spokesman for Christian healing. This change was caused in part by the many healings he saw in Milan, Carthage, and Hippo. Kelsey described this transition as follows:

> The development of Augustine's thought holds special interest for the understanding of Christian healing. He was the preeminent theologian in the West for nearly a thousand years. In his early writings he stated quite specifically that Christians are not to look for continuance of the healing gift. Then something happened, his skepticism gave way to belief in Christ's healing power, and he frankly admitted that he had been wrong. In the *Confessions* he acknowledged the important part played in his conversion by Athanasius'

Life of Anthony. At that time, however, physical healing among the distant desert fathers did not seem important to him. Nearly forty years later in 424, when
his greatest work, *The City of God,* was nearing com-
pletion, his outlook changed. [1]

Augustine's major work, *The City of God,* was written to counter the
widespread pagan accusations that the advent of Christianity and its rejec-
tion of the pagan gods was the cause for the sacking of Rome in 410 by
Visigoth invaders. This highly influential book also contained the author's
philosophy of history and his defense of the concept of predestination.

Certain parts of *The City of God* also included Augustine's explanations of the importance of Christian healing. In Book XXII he presents
some of the most compassionate and moving accounts of spiritual healing
written by any Christian thinker in the entire Middle Ages. In contrast to
his depressing outlook on original sin and predestination, he writes with a
deep warmth and conviction about God's power to heal all kinds of diseases. He implies the dignity of man and his God-given freedom.

Many of the healings cited by Augustine were accomplished by overcoming diseases said to be incurable by the medical profession of the
time. Some of these healings also showed the limitations of medical doctors in the fourth and fifth centuries as well as their lack of a unified
opinion on the proper treatment of various physical maladies.

In his writings on Christian healing, Augustine discussed the signs of
disbelief and opposition to spiritual healing among many people, even
after healings of serious diseases such as cancer. He lamented the tendency of many people to ignore spiritual healing, and he urged that examples of God's healing power be widely publicized to make this important part of Christianity more convincing and more credible. The Bishop
of Hippo strongly praised the practice of reading the accounts of healing
in the Bible to the congregations in churches in North Africa. At this late
stage in his clerical career he realized that spiritual healing provided the
necessary proof of the veracity of Jesus' teachings. Weltin declared:
"Augustine considered miracles necessary to help establish the authority
of the Church, to confirm truth, and to confound heretics." [2]

All of the following readings from Augustine's commentary on Christian healing are from Book XXII in *The City of God.*

The first group discusses the challenge confronting many people in
believing the miracles or marvels recorded in the New Testament. The
most "stupendous" of these miracles, the author states, is the resurrection
and ascension of Jesus Christ. He also discusses one of the most perva-

sive challenges confronting Christian healing in all ages, namely, the doubts and uncertainties of a variety of skeptics.

¶ Those who had not themselves seen Christ rising from the dead and ascending into heaven with His flesh believed the men who said they had seen the miracle, not merely because these men said so, but also because these men themselves worked miracles. For example, many people were astonished to hear these men, who knew but two languages (and, in some cases, only one) suddenly break forth into so many tongues that everybody in the audience understood.

They saw a man who had been lame from earliest infancy now, after forty years, stand upright at a word uttered by these witnesses who spoke in the name of Christ. Pieces of cloth that touched their bodies were found to heal the sick. Uncounted people suffering from various diseases set themselves in line in the street where the Apostles were to pass and where their shadows would fall upon the sick, and many of these people were at once be [sic] restored to health. Besides many other marvels wrought in the name of Christ, there were even cases of dead men restored to life.

Now, those who read such marvels either believe them or they do not. If they believe them, then we can add ever so many incredibilities to the three already mentioned. To gain faith in the one miracle of the Resurrection and Ascension of the flesh into heaven, we literally heap up a mass of testimonies to a multitude of incredibilities. Yet, in spite of all this, we fail to bend to our belief the horrendous hardness of the skeptics' heart.

If, on the other hand, skeptics will not believe that these miracles were wrought through the Apostles precisely for the purpose of making it easier to believe their preaching of the Resurrection and Ascension of Christ, we are still left with the one stupendous miracle, which is all we need: the miracle of the whole world believing, without benefit of miracles, the miracle of the Resurrection. (Chap.5, para. 6, 7)

¶ It is sometimes objected that the miracles, which Christians claim to have occurred, no longer happen. One answer might be that they are no longer needed as they once were to help an unbelieving world to believe. As things now are, any lone believer looking for a miracle to help him to believe, in the midst of a world in which practically everyone already believes, is surely himself a marvel of no mean magnitude.

However, the malice of the objection is in the insinuation that not even the earlier miracles ought to be believed. It is an insinuation that leaves our friends with two facts unexplained: How do they explain that the Ascension of Christ into heaven has come to be everywhere proclaimed with so firm a faith; and how do they explain that our world, which is so advanced in culture and so critical in mentality, has come, without benefit of miracles, to believe so miraculously in realities so incredible?

Perhaps they will say: 'Well, the tales were not wholly incredible and so people came to believe them.' In that case, our friends have still to explain why they themselves have remained so incredulous.

Perhaps it is better to meet such irresponsible skepticism in a summary dilemma which would run as follows: Either the world has founded its faith in an unseen and incredible occurrence on the fact that no less incredible occurrences not merely took place but were seen to take place; or else the original occurrence was so palpably credible that it needed no additional miracles to convince men's minds of its truth.

In either case, our friends are left with no justification of their own willful skepticism. It is simply undeniable that, as a fact, there have been any number of miracles attesting the one, sublime, and saving miracle of Christ's Ascension into heaven with the flesh in which He arose from the dead. The books which record these miracles are absolutely trustworthy and, what is more, they record not merely the attesting of miracles but the ultimate object of our faith which the miracles were meant to confirm.

The miracles were made known to help men's faith and, of course, they are now still better known on account of the faith which the world has embraced. The miracles are read to our people in our churches to nourish their faith, although the people would not be in the churches to hear them read unless the miracles were already believed. (Chap. 8, para. 1, 2)

The second group of readings relates in considerable detail some of the healings witnessed by Augustine in his long clerical career, including healings performed in Milan, Carthage, and Hippo. Many of the healings described in this section involve the use of relics, pilgrimages, and venerations at holy shrines, often the shrines of Christian martyrs. The relics were usually pieces of cloth taken from garments worn by the early martyrs or they were parts (usually bones) of their bodies. This method of healing was widespread in Western Europe and the Mediterranean area throughout the Middle Ages.

As explained in Part One, this method of healing very likely showed a form of faith-healing where people reached out for some religious object or inspirational message that was lacking in local church services and clerical teaching. This use of pilgrimages and relics as a form of Christian worship was curtailed after the Protestant Reformation around 1500.

It is important to note that Augustine also relates many healings that were accomplished without the use of relics or holy shrines. Like the healings achieved by Jesus, the Apostles, the early church, Anthony, and Hilarion, they were accomplished solely by faith, understanding, and prayer. One of the following healings discussed by Augustine (the healing of Innocent, a former government official in Carthage) is the most lengthy and minutely described account of overcoming a serious organic disease recorded by any writer in the Middle Ages. This particular case showed the power of prayer in achieving a remarkable healing in spite of the most advanced medical advice of the time. It also revealed Augustine's own participation and confidence in the process of Christian healing.

¶ The truth is that even today miracles are being wrought in the name of Christ, sometimes through His sacraments and sometimes through the intercession of the relics of His saints. Only, such miracles do not strike the imagination with the same flashing brilliance as the earlier miracles, and so they do not get the same flashing publicity as the others did.

The fact that the canon of our Scriptures is definitely closed brings it about that the original miracles are everywhere repeated and are fixed in people's memory, whereas contemporary miracles which happen here or there seldom become known even to the whole of our local population in and around the place where they occur.

Especially is this the case in the more populous cities, where relatively few learn the facts while most of the people remain uninformed. And when the news does spread from mouth to mouth, even in the case of Christians reporting to Christians, it is too unauthoritative to be received without some difficulty or doubt. (Chap. 8, para. 3)

¶ This, however, was not the case with a miracle that took place in Milan while I was there. A great many people managed to hear of a blind man whose sight was restored because the city is big and, besides, the Emperor was there at the time and an immense multitude of people were gathered to venerate the relics of the martyrs, Protasius and Gervasius, and so witnessed what took place.

The relics had been hidden, and no one knew where they were until the hiding place was revealed in a dream to Bishop Ambrose, who thereupon went and found them. It was on that occasion that the long-enduring darkness dropped from the blind man's eyes and he saw the light of day. (Chap. 8, para. 4)

¶ On the other hand, only a handful of people have ever heard of a cure that occurred in Carthage when I was there and which I witnessed with my own eyes. It happened to Innocent, a former advocate in the office of deputy prefect, at the time when my fellow bishop, Alypius, and I (neither of us yet ordained, but both already dedicated to God) had just returned from Italy.

Innocent, along with his whole household, was a remarkably devout Catholic and he welcomed us into his home. He was just then undergoing medical care in connection with a complicated case of multiple rectal fistula. The doctors had already incised and were now following up with applied medications. The cutting had caused very acute pains and these continued day after day, the trouble being that one of the sinuses that should have been opened was so recessed that it had escaped the scrutiny of the surgeons. Long after all the other sinuses were healed, this single one remained, and all efforts to relieve the patient's pain were unavailing.

Naturally, he became afraid that a second operation would be called for, particularly since his family doctor, who had not been allowed even to watch the original operation, had told Innocent that this would be the case. On that occasion, Innocent had become so annoyed that he dismissed the doctor from his service. His anxiety, however, continued.

One day, in fact, he turned to his surgeons and burst out: 'Do you mean to cut me again? Don't tell me that the man you refused to admit to the operation was right after all!' The surgeons, however, merely scoffed at the family doctor's naivete and tried to calm their patient and, in their best bedside manner, made soothing promises.

But, as day after day dragged on, nothing came of all their medications. The surgeons kept saying that there was no need to operate and that all would respond to treatment. However, they called in for consultation Ammonius, a very old and famous practitioner, who has since died. He examined the patient's rectum and, on the basis of the other surgeons' technique and aftercare, gave the same prognosis as they. Innocent, for the moment, was so assured by the weight of this authority that he began to talk as though he were already cured. He even indulged in cheerful banter at the expense of the poor family doctor who had predicted that more cutting was to come.

Well, to make a long story short, so many days passed to no purpose that the worn-out and humbled surgeons confessed, at last, that nothing short of the scalpel would effect a cure. Poor Innocent turned pale with fear and nearly fainted. As soon as he was sufficiently calm to talk, he told them to get out and never come back again.

Worn out with weeping and with no other recourse, he thought that the best thing he could do would be to call in an extremely skillful surgeon from Alexandria, and have him do what he was too angry to let the other surgeons do. This world-famous specialist came, and examined with his trained eye the excellent work the others had done, as was clear from the healthy residual scar tissue.

Whereupon, the specialist behaved like a man of principle and persuaded Innocent to allow the surgeons to have the satisfaction of terminating a case on which they had obviously worked so well and so long. He admitted that no cure was possible without a second operation, but protested that it would be utterly against his professional ethics to deprive others of the satisfaction of completing an operation in which so little remained to be done and, especially, to deprive men whose skillful work and careful handling of the patient he so much admired.

So the surgeons returned to the good graces of Innocent, and it was agreed that they should incise the remaining sinus in the presence of the Alexandrian specialist. The operation was set for the next day, all the doctors admitting that it was the only way to heal the trouble.

Once they were gone, the whole household set up a wail of grief for their master that was worse than a funeral, and we had the hardest time keeping them calm. Among Innocent's habitual visitors who happened to be there that day were that holy man of blessed memory, Saturninus, then Bishop of Uzalum, and Gulosus, a holy priest, and some deacons of the church at Carthage, one of whom was my highly esteemed friend and now colleague in the episcopate, Aurelius. He is the sole survivor of that group of guests, and I have often compared notes with him regarding this remarkable mercy of God and have found that his memory of the events corresponds with my own.

Their visit, as usual, was in the evening, and Innocent begged them, with tearfulness in his voice, to please come the next day to what, he was sure, would be not merely his agony but his death. The very thought of the previous pains filled him with fear, and he was certain that he would die under the hands of the surgeons. Everyone tried to comfort him, and to exhort him to put his trust in God, and face His will unflinchingly.

Then we all began to pray. The rest of us prayed, as we usually do, on our knees and prostrate on the floor, but Innocent literally threw himself flat as though he had been violently struck by some powerful blow, and then burst into prayer so vehemently, so feelingly, so pathetically and wept with such indescribable groaning and sobbing that he shook in every fiber of his being and all but choked.

How any of the others could pray, with all this pitiable petitioning to distract them, I do not know. As for myself, no formula of prayer was possible. All I could do was let my heart repeat this short refrain: 'Lord, if Thou dost not hear such prayers, what prayers of any saint can move Thee?' It seemed to me that, with one more sigh, the poor man would have prayed himself to death.

At last, we all arose and, when the bishop had given us his blessing, left. There was one final request that all would be present in the morning and, on our part, one last exhortation for the sufferer to have fortitude.

The dreaded day had hardly dawned when all these men of God were at the door to keep their promises. The doctors entered. The needed preparations were

immediately under way. As each piece of frightening
metal flashed, we gasped and held our breath. Then,
while the patient's body was being properly disposed
for the hand of the operating surgeon, Innocent's closest friends stood by, whispering words of comfort to
cheer his drooping spirit.

The bandages were removed. The site was exposed.
The surgeon took a look. With the scalpel in one hand,
he palpated for the offending sinus. He searched once
more with his eye. He probed again with his fingers.
He exhausted every means of medical examination.
But there was nothing to be found except perfectly
healthy tissue!

Imagine the burst of joy and the flood of grateful tears,
the praise and thanks to the God of mercy and of
power, that broke from every one there present. It was
a scene too much for any pen to tell. I can only leave it
to the meditation of my readers. (Chap. 8, para. 5–13)

¶ There was the case, also in Carthage, of Innocentia,
a woman of the highest social standing, and, at the
same time, deeply religious. She was suffering from
cancer of the breast, a malady, as the profession holds,
that yields to no known medical treatment. In the case
of cancer, all that is usually done is to excise completely the portion of the body where the trouble begins, or else, following the opinion of Hippocrates, to
attempt no treatment whatever and so prolong somewhat a life that is already doomed.

Innocentia, accepting the second alternative, on the
advice of an eminent doctor who was a close friend of
the family, betook herself solely to God in prayer.
However, just before Easter, she had a dream, in
which she was told to wait on the women's side of the
baptistry until the first of the newly baptized women
should approach and then ask her to make the sign of
Christ on the affected breast. This she did, and she was
immediately cured.

The doctor who had told her to dispense with all treatment if she cared to live a little longer now examined

the patient and found her completely cured, though his previous examination showed that she was suffering from cancer. Of course, he was all curiosity, and insisted on her telling him what medication she had used. He was dying to find out, if he could, a treatment that would upset the theory of Hippocrates.

When he heard her story, his lips and face expressed nothing but contempt, and she was dreadfully afraid that he was going to break out into some blasphemy against Christ. However, he maintained a religious urbanity and merely observed: 'I had hoped that you might have told me something significant.' Innocentia was shocked by his indifference, but promptly replied: 'Well, for Christ to heal a cancer after He raised to life a man four days dead is not, I suppose, particularly significant.'

Now when the facts reached my ears, I was positively angry that so great a miracle, wrought on a person who was so far from being of no consequence, could happen in a city like Carthage and not be publicized. In fact, I felt it my duty to administer to her an emphatic protest.

She replied that she had not been wholly silent on the matter. However, when I made inquiries among her closest acquaintances, they confessed that they had heard nothing of the affair. I turned on Innocentia and complained: 'This is what you mean, then, by not being wholly silent. You have not mentioned the miracle even to your most intimate friends.'

Then, since she had told me only the outlines of the story, I made her retell it in every detail just as it happened, while her friends, who were there, listened in immense amazement and, when she was done, glorified God. (Chap. 8, para. 14–16)

¶ There was an ex-showman of Curubis who was suffering from paralysis and a bad case of hernia in the scrotum. As soon as he was baptized, both troubles disappeared and he was restored to health. He left the font as sound in body as though he had never been afflicted.

Yet, outside of Curubis, hardly more than a handful of people overheard of the facts which could so easily have been learned. As for myself, as soon as word reached me, I arranged to have Bishop Aurelius send this man to Carthage, even though I had no reason whatever for doubting those who first told me the story. (Chap. 8, para. 18)

¶ There is an estate in the country less than thirty miles from Hippo Regius, called Victoriana. The shrine there is dedicated to the martyrs of Milan, Protasius and Gervasius. To this shrine there was brought a youth who had become possessed by a devil, one summer's day at noon, when he was cooling his horse in the flowing waters of a river.

This demoniac was lying near the altar of the shrine as though he were dead as a corpse, when the lady of the villa came to vespers and evening prayers, as was her wont, along with her maids and some nuns. As soon as they began to sing, the demoniac, as though struck by the sound, came to and, trembling all over, took hold of the altar.

Unable or not daring to move, there he remained, as though he had been tied or fastened to the altar. The demon, crying out at the top of his voice, began to beg for mercy, and to confess where and when he had taken possession of the young man. Finally, the demon declared that he would depart. He did so, but not before threatening to work havoc with certain parts of the young man's body. These parts the demon named. Thereupon, an eye was found torn from its socket. . . . The pupil, which was black, turned white.

Those who had witnessed all this, and others who had been attracted by the screaming, prostrated themselves in prayer. They were overjoyed by the youth's return to sanity, but grieved by the dislocation of the eye. Some insisted that a doctor be called, but the youth's brother-in-law, who had brought him to the shrine, said simply: 'God who put this demon to flight is able, through the prayers of His saints, to restore the sight of this eye.'

Thereupon, as best he could, he pushed the eye back into its socket, bandaged it with his handkerchief, and said that the bandage must not be removed for at least a week. A week later, the bandage was removed. The eye was found to be in perfect condition. Many other miracles occurred at that shrine, but I need not mention them here. (Chap. 8, para. 21 - 22)

¶ At Aquae Tibilitane, there was once a procession in which Bishop Praejectus was carrying a relic of the glorious martyr, St. Stephen, and, while an immense crowd was milling around him, a blind woman begged to be led to the bishop.

She handed him the flowers in her hand. He took them and applied them to her eyes. Immediately she was able to see. Full of joy, she took her place in the procession, needing no one to lead her, and the people followed in amazement behind her. (Chap. 8, para. 25)

Near the end of Book XXII in *The City of God*, Augustine tells of his inability to relate the large number of healing miracles he had witnessed in his travels and in his duties as the Bishop of Hippo. In this part of his classical work he explains the reasons for including this lengthy account of Christian healings in the most important writing of his long and influential career.

¶ Here I am in a fix. I promised to hurry on with the writing of this work. How can I delay to tell all the miracles I know? And on the other hand, I know that many of my fellow Catholics, when they come to read what I have written, will complain that I have left out any number of miracles which they happen to know as well as I do. All I can do is to ask them now to forgive me, and to remember how long a task it would be to tell them and how impossible it would be to do both that and also my duty of bringing this work to an end.

Actually, if I kept merely to miracles of healing and omitted all others, and if I told only those wrought by

this one martyr, the glorious St. Stephen, and if I limited myself to those that happened here at Hippo and
Calama, I should have to fill several volumes and,
even then, I could no more than tell those cases that
have been officially recorded and attested for public
reading in our churches.

This recording and attesting, in fact, is what I took
care to have done, once I realized how many miracles
were occurring in our own day and which were so like
the miracles of old and also how wrong it would be to
allow the memory of these marvels of divine power to
perish from among our people.

It is only two years ago that the keeping of records
was begun here in Hippo, and already, at this writing,
we have nearly seventy attested miracles. I know with
certain knowledge of many others which have not, so
far, been officially recorded. And, of course, at Calama, where the recording began much earlier and
where miracles are more frequent, the number of attested cases is incomparably greater.

So, too, at Uzalum, a town near the city of Utica, there
have been, to my knowledge, many notable miracles
wrought through this same martyr. Thanks to Bishop
Evodius, there was a shrine there dedicated to St.
Stephen long before ours was established. But the custom of taking formal depositions from witnesses was
not there in vogue, nor is to now - unless, perhaps, it
has been very recently introduced.

Not long ago when I was there, a lady of great distinction, Petronia by name, was miraculously cured of a
serious and long-standing sickness which had baffled
the doctors. I urged her, with Bishop Evodius concur-
ring, to have a written deposition drawn up which
could be read in church to the people, and she obedi-
ently accepted the suggestion. (Chap. 8, para. 33 - 35)

¶ It is a simple fact, that there is no lack of miracles
even in our day. And the God who works the miracles
we read of in the Scriptures uses any means and man-

ner He chooses. The only trouble is that these modern miracles are not so well known as the earlier ones, nor are they sufficiently pounded into people's memory by constant reading, so that they may stick, as it were, like gravel in cement.

Even where pains are taken, as is now the case in Hippo, to have the written depositions of the beneficiaries of these graces read to the people, only those in church hear the stories, and that only once, and the many who are not present hear nothing, and those who have listened forget in a day or so, and you hardly ever hear of a person who has heard a deposition telling it to someone else who was not in church for the reading. (Chap. 8, para. 38)

¶ Now, the faith to which all these miracles bear witness is the faith that holds that Christ rose bodily from the dead and ascended with His flesh into heaven, because, of course, the martyrs were witnesses. That, in fact, is what the word 'martyr' means. The martyrs were witnesses to this faith. It was because they bore witness to this faith that they found the world hostile and cruel.

Yet, they overcame the world, not by defending themselves, but by preferring to die for Christ. Those whose intercession has the power from the Lord to work these miracles were killed on account of His name and died for faith in Him. First came the miracle of their fortitude in dying for this faith, and then came, as a consequence, the power revealed in these miracles.

This question, then, calls for an answer: If the resurrection of the flesh into eternal life did not occur in the case of Christ and is not to occur hereafter in our case, in accordance with the promises made by Christ and those in the Old Testament which likewise foretold the coming of Christ, then how explain these great wonders wrought by dead martyrs? For they were put to death precisely for that faith which proclaims this resurrection.

It makes no difference whether we say that it is God Himself who works these miracles in the marvelous way that the Eternal operates in the temporal order, or whether we say that God works these miracles through His servants. And, in regard to what He does through His servants, it is all one whether He does these things through the spirits of martyrs, as though they were still living in their bodies, or whether He uses angels and effects His purposes by His orders, which are given invisibly, inaudibly, immutably.

In that case, miracles which we think are done by martyrs are the result, rather, of their prayers and intercession, and not of their actions. Or God may have varying means to His different ends and these means may be altogether incomprehensible to the minds of men. But the main point is that all miracles are witnesses to that faith which proclaims the supreme miracle of the resurrection of the flesh into life everlasting. (Chap. 9, para. 1, 2)

CHAPTER 4

SULPICIUS SEVERUS

(CIRCA 340 – 420)

Sulpicius Severus was born around 340 into a prominent family in Aquitaine in southwestern France. He was educated at Bordeaux and became a successful lawyer. He married into a wealthy family and began to distinguish himself in public affairs. The sudden death of his wife turned him away from the pursuit of worldly riches and distinction to a life of religion and scholarship.[1] He was baptized in 390 and soon met Martin, the dynamic and influential bishop of Tours. Throughout the remainder of his life, Sulpicius stayed in close association with Martin and his followers.

Sulpicius had no significant role in shaping church doctrine or policy, unlike Athanasius, Jerome, and Augustine. His primary contribution in Christian history was his biography of Martin, titled *The Life of St. Martin* (*Vita S. Martini*). This book contained the record of the works of one of the most important healers in the early church. As an author, Sulpicius remained much less known than the subject of his famous biography. For more than 1500 years *The Life* was widely read throughout the Christian world, yet very few readers knew the author of this important biography. One historian wrote:

> It may well be that there was little in Sulpicius himself to merit personal fame and that, apart from such spiritual heroism as was required for his renunciation of worldly honors, his only great achievement was to produce the portrait of the indefatigable pastor of souls, missioner, monk, and worker of miracles whom chiefly through the pen of Sulpicius, the world knows as Martin of Tours.[2]

In compiling his highly readable book, Sulpicius made a significant contribution to our knowledge of Christian healing during the early Mid-

dle Ages. Like many other early church figures, he did not perform healing works himself. Instead his role was as a recorder of early Christian
healing. In addition to his biography of Martin, Sulpicius wrote a treatise
called *Chronicles,* which was a sacred history of creation up to his own
time. He also wrote an exposition titled *Dialogues,* consisting largely of
a supplement to his life of Martin and a defense against critics skeptical
of the healing works of the widely-known bishop of Tours.

   The first group of readings from *The Life of St. Martin* relates some
of Sulpicius' reasons for writing this biography of a major religious
leader who distinguished himself in performing many remarkable healings. These passages also describe Martin's early life and his change
from military service to a career as a member of the clergy. They reveal that Martin would have preferred the life of a desert father much
like Anthony and Hilarion, but other circumstances caused him to
strengthen the church and establish a healing mission in France and
northern Italy.

> ¶ I thought it would be worth while if I wrote down
> the life of a very holy man, to serve in turn as an ex-
> ample to others. In this way, readers will be spurred on
> to true wisdom, to the heavenly warfaring, and to
> Godlike virtue. In this I am also taking account of my
> own advantage; yet it is not a place in the vain mem-
> ory of men that I expect, but an eternal reward from
> God. Even though my own life has not been such as to
> permit it to be an example to others, I have taken pains
> to see that one who is worthy of imitation should not
> remain in obscurity.
>
> It is, then, the life of St. Martin that I shall begin to
> write, both what preceded his episcopate and what
> happened during it, though I surely shall not be able to
> embrace all the particulars of his career. Indeed, as to
> those events of which he himself was the sole witness,
> we are completely in ignorance. Looking for no praise
> from men, he would have wished to conceal all his
> miracles, insofar as he could.
>
> Even so, among those acts of which I have learned, I
> have omitted many, thinking it sufficient if only the
> outstanding ones should be noted. Consideration for
> my readers requires me at the same time to see to it

that an excessive mass of material should not weary them. I beg those who will read this to give their trust to what has been written, and to believe that I have set down nothing without full knowledge and proof. Rather than tell falsehoods, I should have preferred to be silent. (Chap. 1)

¶ To begin, Martin was a native of Sabaria, a town of the Pannonians, but was reared in Italy, in Ticinum. His parents were not of lowly rank according to worldly standards, but were pagans. His father was first a simple soldier and afterwards military tribune. Martin himself, entering the military service in his youth, served in the cavalry of the imperial guard under Emperor Constantius, and subsequently under Emperor Julian.

Yet this was not of his own accord, for, from almost his first years, he aspired rather to the service of God, his saintly childhood foreshadowing the nobility of his youth. When he was ten years old, against the wish of his parents, he took refuge in a church and demanded to be made a catechumen. With a complete and remarkable dedication to the work of God, he longed, at the age of twelve, for the desert, and would indeed have satisfied his wish if the weakness of his years had not stood in the way. With his spirit, none the less, ever drawn toward monasteries or the Church, he even then in boyhood was reflecting upon what later his devotion was to fulfil.

But, when an imperial edict was issued, requiring the sons of veterans to be enrolled for military service, he was handed over by his father, who was hostile toward his spiritual actions. Martin was fifteen years old when arrested and in chains, he was subjected to the military oath. He satisfied himself with the service of a single slave. Yet, by a reversal of roles, it was the master who was the servant. This went so far that Martin generally took off the other's boots, and cleaned them himself. They would take their meals together, Martin, however, usually doing the serving.

He was three years under arms before his baptism, yet
free from those vices in which such men are commonly
involved. His kindness toward his fellow soldiers was
great, his charity remarkable, and his patience and humility surpassed human measure. There is no need to
praise his temperance; it was such that even he was
considered not a soldier, but a monk. These traits
served so to attach his fellows to him that their remarkable affection for him amounted to veneration.

None the less he had not yet been reborn in Christ, but
was serving a sort of candidacy for baptism through
his good works: assisting the sick, bringing help to the
wretched, feeding the needy, clothing the naked, reserving nothing from his army pay beyond his suste-
nance. With no thought for the morrow, he even then
was not listening with deaf ears to the words of the
Gospel. (Chap. 2)

After leaving military service, Martin was appointed as an exorcist for
the church. He began his clerical career in a monastery near Poitiers
where he performed his first healings. Shortly thereafter he was appointed as the bishop of Tours. Some of the healings cited here involve
similar circumstances as in healings performed by Jesus. This record
shows how tangible proofs of God's healing power have persuaded non-
believers to embrace the Christian church.

¶ It was at this time that there joined him a catechumen eager to be instructed by the discipline of so holy
a man. A few days later, the catechumen was seized
with faintness and fell sick with a violent fever. Martin
happened to be away at the time and after three days'
absence returned to find a lifeless body. Death had
come so suddenly that the catechumen had expired
without being baptized.

The body had been laid out and the sorrowing brothers were busily performing their sad duties upon it,
when Martin came running up, weeping and lament-
ing. Then his whole mind was suffused with the Holy
Spirit. He told all the others to leave the cell in which

the body lay. He barred the door and stretched himself upon the lifeless body of the dead brother.

For some time he gave himself to prayer and perceived through the Spirit that the virtue of the Lord was present. Lifting himself up somewhat and with his gaze fixed upon the face of the dead man, he awaited with confidence the outcome of his own prayers and of the mercy of the Lord.

Hardly two hours had elapsed before he saw all the limbs of the dead man move little by little and his eyes quiver as they opened, once more to see. Then, turning to the Lord with a loud voice and giving thanks, Martin filled the whole cell with his cry of joy. On hearing this, those who had been standing outside the door at once rushed in. Wonderful spectacle: they saw alive one whom they had abandoned as dead. The catechumen, restored to life, at once received baptism and lived for many years afterwards: he, indeed, was the first to furnish us proof or tangible evidence of Martin's miracles. (Chap. 7)

¶ Not long afterwards, while Martin was going across the property of a certain Lupicinus, a man of distinguished worldly position, the grief-stricken cries of a throng of mourners caught his ear. Martin was concerned at this, and approached. Asking what the mourning was, he was told one of the household, a young slave, had taken his own life by hanging.

On learning this, Martin entered the cell where the body lay. He cleared the room of the thronging spectators and, stretching himself upon the body, prayed for a while. Soon, life began to return to the features of the dead man, as his still languid eyes were lifted to look into the face of Martin.

Forcing himself slowly to rise and grasping the hand of the blessed man, he stood up. Then, accompanied by Martin as the whole crowd looked on, he walked to the vestibule of the house. (Chap. 8)

¶ In the matter of healing, Martin had such a power of grace within him that hardly anyone who was sick approached him without at once recovering health. A clear example will be found in the following incident.

At Treves, a girl lay ill in the grip of a fearful paralysis. For a long time she could make no use of her body for the needs of human life. Already dead in all her members, her body breathed feebly and barely pulsed with life. Her kin were standing by, awaiting only her funeral, when suddenly the news was brought that Martin had come to that city.

When the girl's father learned this, he ran breathlessly to beseech him on behalf of his daughter. As it happened, Martin had already entered the church. There, under the eyes of the people and in the presence of many other bishops, the old man, waiting, embraced his knees and said: 'My daughter is dying from a terrible kind of sickness. Her condition is more cruel than death itself: it is only through breathing that she lives; in her flesh she is already dead. I beg you to come to her and bless her, for I have faith that she can be restored to health through you.'

These words confused and astonished Martin, and he drew back, saying that the grace required for such an act was not his. The old man's judgment had misled him, he said; he was unworthy to be an agent for the manifestation of the Lord's power. The father persisted, weeping more bitterly and praying him to visit the lifeless girl.

Finally, the bishops who stood about compelled him to go, and he went down to the girl's house. A great crowd was waiting before the door to see what the servant of God would do. Using the means which were familiar to him in situations of this kind, he first prostrated himself upon the floor and prayed.

Then he looked at the sick girl and asked that some oil be given him. He blessed the potent and sanctified fluid and poured it into the girl's mouth. At once, her voice was restored to her. Then, at his touch, her members one by one began gradually to regain life, until, with the people there to witness it, strength returned to the limbs and she arose. (Chap. 16)

¶ In the same period, a slave of a certain proconsul, Taetradius, had been possessed by a demon and was suffering terrible torture. Martin, asked to lay his hand upon him, ordered that the man be brought to him. The evil spirit, however, could in no way be brought out of the little room where he was; against those who came near he raged and bared his teeth. Then, Taetradius threw himself at the knees of the blessed man and begged him to go down to the house where the possessed man was. At this, Martin said that he could not come to the house of a profane and pagan person (for Taetradius was at that time still entangled in the error of paganism). So, Taetradius promised to become a Christian if the demon should be driven out of the boy.

Martin then laid his hand upon the boy and expelled the unclean spirit. When Taetradius saw this, he believed in the Lord Jesus. He was made a catechumen at once and not long afterwards was baptized. Since it was to Martin that he attributed his salvation, he always showed him a wonderful affection.

In the same town and at about the same time, Martin, on entering the dwelling of a certain householder, halted at the very threshold, saying that he saw a horrible demon in the vestibule of the house. When Martin ordered him to depart, he took possession of the householder's cook, who stayed in the inner part of the house.

The wretched man madly began to bite and to lacerate whoever confronted him. The household was alarmed, the slaves thrown into confusion, the people reduced to flight. Martin threw himself before the maniac and, first, ordered him to stand still. When the other gnashed his teeth and, with mouth agape, threatened to bite him, Martin thrust his fingers into his mouth. 'If you have any power,' he said, 'bite these.'

Then, as if he had taken a white-hot iron in his throat, the possessed man drew back his teeth so as to avoid touching the fingers of the blessed man. The pains and tortures he was suffering were forcing the demon to leave the possessed body, yet he could not get out through the mouth. So, leaving behind a track of filth, he was expelled in a discharge from the bowels. (Chap. 17)

¶ At Paris, while Martin, accompanied by vast crowds, was entering a gate of the city, he saw a leper. The others all were moved to horror by the leper's lamentable appearance, but Martin kissed him and blessed him. Instantly, he was completely cleansed, and the next day, his skin glistening clear, he came to the church and gave thanks for the recovery of his health.

Mention also should be made of the fact that threads removed from Martin's clothing or hair shirt worked frequent cures upon the sick. Twisted about the fingers or placed on the neck, these fibres frequently expelled illness from diseased bodies. (Chap. 18)

¶ Arborius, the former prefect, a pious and God-fearing man, had a daughter who suffered from the burning heat of a quartan fever. A letter from Martin had been brought to him by chance. This letter, when the fever was again intense, he placed on the girl's chest; instantly, the fever departed.

The event had such an effect on Arborius that he at once promised the girl to God and dedicated her to perpetual virginity. He then went to Martin and presented to him the girl who had been cured through him, even though he was absent — a visible witness of his miraculous powers. Arborius would not have it otherwise than that she should receive the habit of virginity from Martin himself and be consecrated by him.

Paulinus, a man whose example was destined to be very powerful, was undergoing severe pain in one of his eyes, the pupil already covered by a thick film. Martin touched his eye with a little sponge. The pain passed completely away and he was restored to his former health.

One day, Martin chanced somehow or other to fall from an upper story. Tumbling down the rough steps of the stairway, he injured himself in several places. He lay nearly lifeless in his cell under the tortures of excessive pain. In the night he saw an angel wash his wounds and anoint the bruises on his mangled body with a healing ointment. On that day following, he had been so restored to health that you would have thought he had received no harm at all.

But it would be tedious to relate the miracles one by one. Let these suffice, even though they be few among many. And we must be satisfied if, in presenting the more outstanding, we have not detracted from the truth and have at the same time avoided being tedious by offering too many. (Chap. 19)

In his conclusion, Sulpicius tells more about Martin's thought and conduct that made possible his many impressive healings. This final commentary illustrates how Christian healing is inextricably related to a sense of love, conviction, forbearance, and patience.

¶ When I had heard Martin's faith, his career, and miraculous power spoken of for a considerable time, and I was consumed with a longing to know him, I was very glad to undertake a long journey to go and see him. Further, because I already had an ardent desire to write his life, I informed myself by searching out the fact, partly from Martin himself (insofar as he could be questioned), partly from those who had shared his experiences with him or knew about them.

One cannot imagine the humility and kindness with which he received me at that time. He congratulated himself and greatly rejoiced in the Lord that my esteem of him had been such that I had undertaken a long journey to seek him out. Imagine my distress when — I almost dare not confess it — he deigned to invite me to his own saintly board, poured water himself upon my hands and at evening washed my feet. I had not the courage to resist or oppose him.

His authority so overwhelmed me that I thought it sacrilege not to yield to him. In his conversation with me he talked only of the need of abandoning the seductions of the world and the burdens of this present age so that we might follow the Lord Jesus, free and unimpeded.

As the most outstanding example of these times he brought forward that of the illustrious Paulinus, who has been named above. Casting away an incomparable fortune and following Christ, he, almost alone in these times, had carried out the precepts of the Gospel. It was he, he declared, whom we should follow and whom we should imitate.

Our present age was happy in having had such a lesson in faith and virtue. Following the Lord's saying, one who was rich and of many possessions had sold all and had given to the poor. What had seemed impossible to achieve he had made possible through his example.

And in Martin's words and conversation what seriousness, what dignity! How penetrating, how forceful he was, how quick and at ease in resolving questions from the Scriptures! And because I know that many are incredulous on this point (since I have noticed that they do not believe when I myself was telling them about it), I call to witness Jesus and our common hope of salvation that I have never heard from any other mouth words so full of wisdom and of so sound and pure an eloquence. To be sure, in comparison with Martin's virtues, this is but a small commendation, except that it is remarkable that not even this merit was lacking in a man untrained in letters. (Chap. 25)

¶ But now, our book demands an ending; our recital must come to a close. It is not that I have exhausted all that could be said about Martin. Rather, like unskillful poets who become negligent at the end of their work, we are overcome by the mass of our material and leave off. An attempt to speak of his deeds might or might not be successful, but it is otherwise with his interior life, his daily manner of living, the constant direction of his spirit to heaven.

As to these things, I speak the simple truth when I say that no possible form of speech can ever unfold them. His perseverance and temperance in fasts and abstinence, his power in vigils and prayers, nights spent by him as if they were days, with never a moment withdrawn from the work of God, no allowance made for leisure or business, nor even for food or sleep, except insofar as natural necessity compelled him — all this, in very truth, not Homer himself could describe, even if, as they say, he should rise from the dead. So true it is that with Martin everything is too big for words to be able to express it.

An hour, a moment never passed without Martin being absorbed in prayer or busy in reading. Even in the midst of reading or whatever he happened to be doing, he never relaxed his spirit from prayer. Even as blacksmiths, in the midst of their work, try to find some alleviation of their toil by constant striking of the anvil, so Martin, even when he seemed to be doing something else, was always praying.

O truly happy man, in whom there was no guile, who judged no one, who condemned no one, who returned to no one evil for evil! He showed such patience toward all kinds of injury that, though he was highest in dignity, a bishop, even the lowest clergy could abuse him with impunity. Yet, he never on this account removed such men from their posts or, so far as it rested with him, banished them from his love. (Chap. 26)

He was never seen to be angry, never violent, never sorrowing, never laughing. Always one and the same, he seemed, somehow beyond the nature of man, to show a heavenly gladness in his countenance. In his speech, only Christ was ever to be found; in his heart, only love, peace, and mercy.

He would often weep even for the sins of those who had shown themselves his detractors, who used poisoned tongues and viper's teeth to slander him in the quiet of his retreat. Indeed, we have seen at work some who were envious of his virtue and mode of life, who hated in him what they did not see in themselves and could not imitate. And it is a horrible thing, grievous, and lamentable, that there were named as his persecutors — very few though these be — almost no others than bishops.

There is no need to mention any by name, even if most of them will bark out their rage against me. If any of them read this and recognize themselves, it will be enough for me if they are ashamed. If they become angry, that in itself will be an admission that my words concern them, when, perhaps, I was thinking of others. Yet, I do not shrink from having any persons of this sort make me, along with such a man as Martin, the object of their hate.

Of one thing I am reasonably confident, that this little book will find favor with all who are truly faithful. But if anyone reads these things with other than the eyes of faith, the sin will be his own. For myself, I am sure that what led me to write was belief in the story and love of Christ. I am sure, also, that I have related attested facts and spoken the truth. The reward which I hope has been made ready by God will be won, not by him who has read, but by him who has believed. (Chap. 27)

CHAPTER 5

HEALERS IN THE
EASTERN ORTHODOX CHURCH

(FOURTH AND FIFTH CENTURIES)

A distinctive form of Christianity and Christian healing began to emerge during the fourth and fifth centuries in the eastern region of the crumbling Roman Empire. Constantinople became the major Christian capital, and for several hundred years it assumed a preeminent role in shaping Christian theology. The new Byzantine empire reached its highest influence under Emperor Justinian (527 – 565), and it gradually moved away from Western Christendom in doctrine and religious practices. [1]

Relations between the two branches of Christianity became increasingly strained, and in 1054 their leaders mutually excommunicated each other from the "official" church. The split became final in 1204 when the armies of the Fourth Crusade coming from Western Europe sacked and temporarily occupied Constantinople. At this time Christianity was divided into two separate churches: the Roman Catholic Church and the Eastern Orthodox Church. The Eastern church was greatly weakened when Moslem Turks conquered Constantinople in 1453 and started the Ottoman Empire. During its long struggle with the Western church and other opponents, Eastern Orthodoxy spread its influence into Russia, the Ukraine, Romania, and Bulgaria.

Early leaders in the Eastern Orthodox church contributed some of the major writings on Christian doctrine as well as important accounts of Christian healing. Three important patriarchs were the Cappadocian Fathers: Basil the Great (329 – 379), Gregory of Nazianzen (329 – 389), and Gregory of Nyssa (331 – 396), the younger brother of Basil. [2] One of the most important church historians was Socrates Scholasticus (380 – 445).

From its beginning, Eastern Orthodoxy has relied heavily on prayer for healing the sick, and at the same time it has included the use of medical practitioners. The concept and practice of healing makes explicit reference to the use of medicine and doctors. This idea has been well stated in *Ecclesiasticus,* a book not included in some versions of the Scriptures.

> My son, in thy sickness be not negligent: but pray to the Lord, and he will make thee whole. Leave off from sin, and order thy hands aright, and cleanse thy heart from all wickedness. Give a sweet savour, and a memorial of fine flour; and make a fat offering. Then give place to the physician, for the Lord hath created him: let him not go from thee, for thou hast need of him. There is a time when in their hands there is good success. For they shall also pray unto the Lord, that he would prosper that which they give for ease and remedy to prolong life. (38: 9 – 14)

However, the Eastern Orthodox church throughout its history has placed God and prayer in a superior position in the process of healing disease. An eminent historian of medicine and religion in early Christianity stated:

> Medicines and the skills of physicians are blessings from God. It is not *eo ipso* wrong for a Christian to employ them, but it is sinful to put one's faith in them entirely since, when they are effective, it is only because their efficacy comes from God who can heal without them. Thus to resort to physicians without first placing one's trust in God is both foolish and sinful.[3]

The close relationship between religion and medicine encouraged the Eastern Orthodox church to establish the first hospitals in Europe in the fourth century.[4]

Some healers in the Eastern Orthodox church during the sixth and seventh centuries opposed the use of medicine and relied entirely on spiritual means for healing. St. Theodore of Sykeon, a leader of the church during this period, once declared:

> Have done with doctors. Don't fall into their clutches; you will get no help from them. Be satisfied with prayer and blessing and you will be completely restored to health.[5]

Other spokesmen in the Eastern church also upheld the practice of healing using only faith and prayer. The healings recorded by these early fathers revealed a sense of complete confidence in the healing power of God. This view evidently continued among a portion of the followers of the Eastern Orthodox tradition. Professor Stanley Harakas has stated:

> Throughout the History of Byzantium a minority
> voice minimized the value of rational medicine, pre-
> ferring to trust only in God and his saints for healing.
> Nevertheless, this was not true of the mainline practice
> and teaching in the church. [6]

The Eastern church, unlike its counterpart in the West, never experienced a decline in the use of spiritual healing based on the Bible. Since the fourth century the healing rite described in James' epistle (5: 13 – 16) has continued intact within the liturgical services of the church. The laity have always played an important role in this process. It has never become a formal ritual like the Rite of Extreme Unction in the Western medieval church to prepare a sick or suffering Christian for death. For this reason it has been called the Rite of Holy Unction. Harakas has explained this practice by quoting an author in the Slavic Orthodox tradition as follows:

> The idea that a priest should be called only when
> someone is in danger of death is not an Orthodox idea.
> . . . The priest does not come to prepare a person for
> the grave but he comes to bring spiritual life. Holy
> Unction is a service for the spiritual and physical
> health of an individual. [7]

Gregory of Nazianzen

One of the earliest accounts of healing in the Eastern church was written by Gregory of Nazianzen, a close associate of Basil, the famous bishop of Caesarea (the capital of Cappadocia.) Gregory was later appointed by Basil as the bishop of a small town named Sasina. In 381 Gregory became the bishop of Constantinople, a position he held for only a short time because of bitter attacks from many proponents of Arianism.

Gregory 's major writings consisted of the contents of forty-five orations. The Five Theological Orations that he delivered in Constantinople comprised a strong defense of orthodox Christianity that won him the title of "The Theologian." [8] His works also included descriptions of healings performed by prominent Christians. These healings were accomplished by the use of prayer and an understanding of the relationship between God and man. They often revealed the inability of the medical doctors of the time to heal sickness and disease.

The first of the following passages are Gregory's account of two healing incidents involving Basil. In the first incident, Basil temporarily healed the son of the Arian emperor, Valens, who was about to banish the Christian bishop into exile. Physicians were unable to heal the child, and Basil began restoring him to health. Yet the emperor continued an effort to heal his son with the aid of his physicians and the child died.

> ¶ This was the series of events: the Emperor's child was sick and in bodily pain. The father was pained for it, for what can the father do? On all sides he sought for aid in his distress, he summoned the best physicians, he betook himself to intercessions with the greatest fervour, and flung himself upon the ground. Affliction humbles even emperors, and no wonder, for the like sufferings of David in the case of his child are recorded for us.

> But as no cure for the evil could anywhere be found, he applied to the faith of Basil, not personally summoning him, in shame for his recent ill treatment, but entrusting the mission to others of his nearest and dearest friends. On his arrival, without the delay or reluctance which any one else might have shown, at once the disease relaxed, and the father cherished better hopes; and had he not blended salt water with the fresh, by trusting to the heterodox at the same time that he summoned Basil, the child would have recovered his health and been preserved for his father's arms. This indeed was the conviction of those who were present at the time and shared in the distress. (*Oration XLIII*, The Panegyric on S. Basil, 54.)

The second account by Gregory of Nazianzen relates the healing of a local prefect by Basil after they had had a bitter personal dispute. The prefect's intense physical pain caused him to appeal to Basil and to regret his animosity. This healing shows that a sense of humility and love can help in achieving a restoration of normal physical health. The prelate mentioned in this incident was Basil.

¶ The same mischance is said to have befallen the prefect. He also was obliged by sickness to bow beneath the hands of the Saint, and, in reality, to men of sense a visitation brings instruction, and affliction is often better than prosperity. He fell sick, was in tears, and in pain, he sent for Basil, and entreated him, crying out, "I own that you were in the right; only save me!" His request was granted, as he himself acknowledged, and convinced many who had known nothing of it; for he never ceased to wonder at and describe the powers of the prelate. Such was his conduct in these cases, such its results. (*Ibid.* 55)

The next passages are an account written by Gregory of Nazianzen about the recovery of his own father from a serious illness at the Easter season. In this case the efforts of the physicians were of no use in alleviating the disease. The healing was accomplished, Gregory writes, by appealing in prayer to God, the Great Physician.

¶ Well, he was sick, the time was the holy and illustrious Easter, the queen of days, the brilliant night which dissipates the darkness of sin, upon which without abundant light we keep the feast of our salvation, putting ourselves to death along with the Light once put to death for us, and rising again with Him who rose.

This was the time of his sufferings. Of what kind they were, I will briefly explain. His whole frame was on fire with an excessive, burning fever, his strength had failed, he was unable to take food, his sleep had departed from him, he was in the greatest distress, and agitated by palpitations. Within his mouth, the palate and the whole of the upper surface was so completely and painfully ulcerated, that it was difficult and dangerous to swallow even water.

The skill of physicians, the prayers, most earnest though they were, of his friends, and every possible attention were alike of no avail. He himself in this desperate condition, while his breath came short and fast, had no perception of present things, but was entirely

absent, immersed in the objects he had long desired,
now made ready for him.

We were in the temple, mingling supplications with
the sacred rites, for, in despair of all others, we had be-
taken ourselves to the Great Physician, to the power of
that night, and to the last succour, with the intention,
shall I say, of keeping a feast, or of mourning; of holding festival, or paying funeral honours to one no
longer here? O those tears! which were shed at that
time by all the people. O voices, and cries, and hymns
blended with the psalmody!

From the temple they sought the priest, from the sacred rite the celebrant, from God their worthy ruler,
with my Miriam to lead them and strike the timbrel
not of triumph, but of supplication; learning then for
the first time to put to shame by misfortune, and calling at once upon the people and upon God; upon the
former to sympathize with her distress, and to be lav-
ish of their tears, upon the latter, to listen to her petitions, as, with the inventive genius of suffering, she re-
hearsed before Him all His wonders of old time.

What then was the response of Him who was the God
of that night and of the sick man? A shudder comes
over me as I proceed with my story. And though you,
my hearers, may shudder, do not disbelieve: for that
would be impious, when I am the speaker, and in reference to him. The time of the mystery was come, and
the reverend station and order, when silence is kept for
the solemn rites; and then he was raised up by Him
who quickened the dead, and by the holy night.

At first he moved slightly, then more decidedly; then
in a feeble and indistinct voice he called by name one
of the servants who was in attendance upon him, and
bade him come, and bring his clothes, and support him
with his hand. He came in alarm, and gladly waited
upon him, while he, leaning upon his hand as upon a
staff, imitates Moses upon the mount, arranges his feeble hands in prayer, and in union with, or on behalf of,

his people eagerly celebrates the mysteries, in such few words as his strength allowed, but, as it seems to me, with a most perfect intention.

What a miracle! In the sanctuary without a sanctuary, sacrificing without an altar, a priest far from the sacred rites: yet all these were present to him in the power of the spirit, recognised by him, though unseen by those who were there. Then, after adding the customary words of thanksgiving, and after blessing the people, he retired again to his bed, and after taking a little food, and enjoying a sleep, he recalled his spirit, and, his health being gradually recovered, on the new day of the feast, as we call the first Sunday after the festival of the Resurrection, he entered the temple and inaugurated his life which had been preserved, with the full complement of clergy, and offered the sacrifice of thanksgiving.

To me this seems no less remarkable than the miracle in the case of Hezekiah, who was glorified by God in his sickness and prayers with an extension of life, and this was signified by the return to the shadow of the degrees, according to the request of the king who was restored, whom God honoured at once by the favour and the sign, assuring him of the extension of his days by the extension of the day. (*Oration XVIII*, On the Death of his Father, 28, 29.)

Gregory of Nyssa

Gregory of Nyssa was a younger brother of Basil who achieved a much lesser role in the administration of the church. Unlike Gregory of Nazianzen, he was not a major statesman or preacher. He came into Christianity gradually, and for a time he was a student of rhetoric.

Yet Gregory of Nyssa was perhaps the most penetrating and original thinker of the three Cappadocian Fathers. He wrote brilliantly in defense of the Trinity and other doctrines of orthodox Christianity. One of his greatest interests was writing on the Christian concept of man as belonging to the eternal world and as knowing himself to be God's image and likeness. Payne wrote: "Of the three Cappadocian Fathers Gregory of

Nyssa is the one closest to us, the least proud, the most subtle, the one most committed to the magnificence of man." [9]

The first passages by Gregory of Nyssa are from his treatise *On the Making of Man*. This brief chapter extolling man's beauty and God's love is titled "That man is a likeness of the Divine sovereignty."

> ¶ It is true, indeed, that the Divine beauty is not adorned with any shape or endowment of form, by any beauty of colour, but is contemplated as excellence in unspeakable bliss. As then painters transfer human forms to their pictures by the means of certain colours, laying on their copy the proper and corresponding tints, so that the beauty of the original may be accurately transferred to the likeness, so I would have you understand that our Maker also, painting the portrait to resemble His own beauty, by the addition of virtues, as it were with colours, shows in us His own sovereignty: and manifold and varied are the tints, so to say, by which His true form is portrayed:

> Not red, or white, or the blending of these, whatever it may be called, nor a touch of black that paints the eyebrow and the eye, and shades, by some combination, the depressions in the figure, and all such arts which the hands of painters contrive, but instead of these, purity, freedom from passion, blessedness, alienation from all evil, and all those attributes of the like kind which help to form in men the likeness of God: with such hues as these did the Maker of His own image mark our nature.

> And if you were to examine the other points also by which the Divine beauty is expressed, you will find that to them too the likeness in the image which we present is perfectly preserved. The Godhead is mind and word: for "in the beginning was the Word," and the followers of Paul "have the mind of Christ" which "speaks" in them: humanity too is not far removed from these: you see in yourself word and understanding, an imitation of the very Mind and Word.

> Again, God is love, and the fount of love: for this the great John declares, that "love is of God," and "God is

love:" the Fashioner of our nature has made this to be
our feature too: for "hereby," He says, "shall all men
know that ye are my disciples, if ye love one another":
— thus, if this be absent, the whole stamp of the likeness is transformed. The Deity beholds and hears all
things, and searches all things out: you too have the
power of apprehension of things by means of sight and
hearing, and the understanding that inquires into
things and searches them out. (V: 1, 2)

The next excerpts are also from Gregory of Nyssa's work *On the Making of Man.* They explain in vivid form the gradual elevation of Jesus'
healing mission by his successive victories over death: first by healing
Simon's wife's mother and the nobleman's son, both of whom were on
the brink of death; second by restoring Jairus' daughter after her death;
third by raising the young son of a widow at Nain; and finally by raising
Lazarus from the grave.

Gregory concludes that God most certainly has the power to heal disease, since through Jesus' works He has clearly shown His power over
death. The individual acts of overcoming death are done to prepare "for
men the way of faith in the resurrection." These deeds lead up to the
most convincing healing of all time, the resurrection of Jesus himself
from the tomb three days after his crucifixion.

Gregory imparts a highly sensitive and human account of these familiar Bible incidents. He also adds some meaningful insights into these
demonstrations of Jesus' unexcelled healing ability.

¶ Still more, however, is this the case with the experience of actual resurrection which we have learnt not
so much by words as by actual facts: for as the marvel
of resurrection was great and passing belief, He begins
gradually by inferior instances of His miraculous
power, and accustoms our faith, as it were, for the re-
ception of the greater.

For as a mother who nurses her babe with due care for
a time supplies milk by her breast to its mouth while
still tender and soft; and when it begins to grow and
have teeth she gives it bread, not hard or such as it
cannot chew, so that the tender and unpractised gums
may not be chafed by rough food; but softening it with
her own teeth, she makes it suitable and convenient for

the powers of the eater; and then as its power increases by growth she gradually leads on the babe, accustomed to tender food, to more solid nourishment.

So the Lord, nourishing and fostering with miracles the weakness of the human mind, like some babe not fully grown, makes first of all a prelude of the power of the resurrection in the case of a desperate disease, which prelude, though it was great in its achievement, yet was not such a thing that the statement of it would be disbelieved: for by "rebuking the fever" which was fiercely consuming Simon's wife's mother, He produced so great a removal of the evil as to enable her who was already expected to be near death, to "minister" to those present.

Next He makes a slight addition to the power, and when the nobleman's son lies in acknowledged danger of death (for so the history tells us, that he was about to die, as his father cried, "come down, ere my child die"), He again brings about the resurrection of one who was believed about to die; accomplishing the miracle with a greater act of power in that He did not even approach the place, but sent life from afar by the force of His command.

Once more in what follows He ascends to higher wonders. For having set out on His way to the ruler of the synagogue's daughter, he voluntarily made a halt in His way, while making public the secret cure of the woman with an issue of blood, that in this time death might overcome the sick. When, then, the soul had just been parted from the body, and those who were wailing over the sorrow were making a tumult with their mournful cries, He raises the damsel to life again, as if from sleep, by His word of command, leading on human weakness, by a sort of path and sequence, to greater things.

Still in addition to these acts He exceeds them in wonder, and by a more exalted act of power prepares for men the way of faith in the resurrection. The Scripture tells us of a city called Nain in Judea: a widow there had an only child, no longer a child in the sense of being among boys, but already passing from childhood to man's estate: the narrative calls him "a young man."

The story conveys much in few words: the very recital is a real lamentation: the dead man's mother, it says "was a widow." See you the weight of her misfortune, how the text briefly sets out the tragedy of her suffering? for what does the phrase mean? that she had no more hope of bearing sons, to cure the loss she had just sustained in him who had departed; for the woman was a widow: she had not in her power to look to another instead of to him who was gone; for he was her only child; and how great a grief is here expressed any one may easily see who is not an utter stranger to natural feeling.

Him alone she had known in travail, him alone she had nursed at her breast; he alone made her table cheerful, he alone was the cause of brightness in her home, in play, in work, in learning, in gaiety, at processions, at sports, at gatherings of youth; he alone was all that is sweet and precious in a mother's eyes. Now at the age of marriage, he was the stock of her race, the shoot of its succession, the staff of her old age.

Moreover, even the additional detail of his time of life is another lament: for he who speaks of him as "a young man" tells of the flower of his faded beauty, speaks of him as just covering his face with down, not yet with a full thick beard, but still bright with the beauty of his cheeks. What then, think you, were his mother's sorrows for him? how would her heart be consumed as it were with a flame; how bitterly would she prolong her lament over him, embracing the corpse as it lay before her, lengthening out her mourning for him as far as possible, so as not to hasten the funeral of the dead, but to have her fill of sorrow!

Nor does the narrative pass this by: for Jesus "when He saw her," it says, "had compassion;" "and He came and touched the bier; and they that bare him stood

still;" and He said to the dead, "Young man, I say unto
thee, arise," "and He delivered him to his mother"
alive. Observe that no short time had intervened since
the dead man had entered upon that state, he was all
but laid in the tomb; the miracle wrought by the Lord
is greater, though the command is the same.

His miraculous power proceeds to a still more exalted
act, that its display may more closely approach that
miracle of the resurrection which men doubt. One of
the Lord's companions and friends is ill (Lazarus is
the sick man's name); and the Lord deprecates any
visiting of His friend, though far away from the sick
man, that in the absence of Life, death might find
room and power to do his own work by the agency of
disease.

The Lord informs His disciples in Galilee of what has
befallen Lazarus, and also of his own setting out to
him to raise him up when laid low. They, however,
were exceeding afraid on account of the fury of the
Jews, thinking it a difficult and dangerous matter to
turn again towards Judea, in the midst of those who
sought to slay Him: and thus, lingering and delaying,
they return slowly from Galilee: but they do return, for
His command prevailed, and the disciples were led by
the Lord to be initiated at Bethany in the preliminary
mysteries of the general resurrection.

Four days had already passed since the event; all due
rites had been performed for the departed; the body
was hidden in the tomb: it was probably already
swollen and beginning to dissolve into corruption, as
the body mouldered in the dank earth and necessarily
decayed: the thing was one to turn from, as the dis-
solved body under the constraint of nature changed to
offensiveness.

At this point the doubted fact of the general resurrection is brought to proof by a more manifest miracle;
for one is not raised from severe sickness, nor brought
back to life when at the last breath — nor is a child

just dead brought to life, nor a young man about to be conveyed to the tomb released from his bier; but a man past the prime of life, a corpse, decaying, swollen, yea already in a state of dissolution, so that even his own kinfolk could not suffer that the Lord should draw near the tomb by reason of the offensiveness of the decayed body there enclosed, brought into life by a single call, confirms the proclamation of the resurrection, that is to say, that expectation of it as universal, which we learn by a particular experience to entertain.

For as in the regeneration of the universe the Apostle tells us that "the Lord Himself will descend with a shout, with the voice of the archangel," and by a trumpet sound raise up the dead to incorruption — so now too he who is in the tomb, at the voice of command, shakes off death as if it were a sleep, and ridding himself from the corruption that had come upon his condition of a corpse, leaps forth from the tomb whole and sound, not even hindered in his egress by the bonds of the grave-clothes round his feet and hands.

Are these things too small to produce faith in the resurrection of the dead? or dost thou seek that thy judgment on this point should be confirmed by yet other proofs? In truth the Lord seems to me not to have spoken in vain to them of Capernaum, when He said to Himself, as in the person of men, "Ye will surely say unto me this proverb, 'Physician, heal thyself.'" For it behoved Him, when He had accustomed men to the miracle of the resurrection in other bodies, to confirm His word in His own humanity.

Thou sawest the thing proclaimed working in others — those who were about to die, the child which had just ceased to live, the young man at the edge of the grave, the putrefying corpse, all alike restored by one command to life. Dost thou seek for those who have come to death by wounds and bloodshed? does any feebleness of life-giving power hinder the grace in them? . . .

Since, then, every prediction of the Lord is shown to
be true by the testimony of events, while we not only
have learnt this by His words, but also received the
proof of the promise in deed, from those very persons
who returned to life by resurrection, what occasion is
left to those who disbelieve? Shall we not bid farewell
to those who pervert our simple faith by "philosophy
and vain deceit," and hold fast to our confession in its
purity, learning briefly through the prophet the mode
of grace, by his words, "Thou shalt take away their
breath and they shall fail, and turn to their dust. Thou
shalt send forth Thy Spirit and they shall be created,
and Thou shalt renew the face of the earth;" at which
time also he says that the Lord Rejoices in His works,
sinners having perished from the earth: for how shall
any one be called by the name of sin, when sin itself
exists no longer? (XXV, 6 – 13)

The final selection is from Gregory's writing titled *The Life of St.
Macrina*. It comprises an account of a remarkable healing of the daughter of Sebastopolis, a military officer in charge of a garrison of soldiers in
a district of Cappadocia. This healing was done by Macrina, the older
sister of Gregory, who won a wide reputation for her piety and good
works. It is one of the first recorded healings achieved by a woman in the
annals of Christianity. Macrina is referred to in this account as "the holy
one," "the blessed one," and "the great lady."

The healing of the small girl involves a new concept of medicine, a
"true medicine that heals diseases" and "that comes from prayer." At the
time of this healing Macrina was residing in a monastery headed by Gregory's younger brother named Peter. The incident is told directly to Gregory by the father, Sebastopolis.

¶ There was with us our little girl who was suffering
from an eye ailment resulting from an infectious sickness. It was a terrible and pitiful thing to see her as the
membrane around the pupil was swollen and whitened
by the disease. As we entered the monastery, we separated, my wife and I, for I went to the men's quarters
where your brother Peter was Superior, and she went
to the women's quarters to be with the holy one.

After an interval of time, we thought it was the hour
for us to go home. We were getting ready to leave, but

a kindly remonstrance came to us from both quarters. Your brother urged me to remain and share the monastic table. The blessed one would not let my wife go, and said she would not give up my daughter, whom she was holding in her arms, until she had given them a meal and offered them the wealth of philosophy.

She kissed the child as one might expect and put her lips on her eyes and, when she noticed the diseased pupil, she said: "If you do me the favor of remaining for dinner, I will give you a return in keeping for this honour." When the child's mother asked what it was, the great lady replied: "I have some medicine which is especially effective in curing eye diseases." When a message came to me from the women's quarters about this promise, we gladly remained and disregarded the urgent necessity of starting on our way.

When the feasting was over and grace said (the great Peter, having entertained and cheered us with special graciousness, and the great Macrina, having said goodbye to my wife with every courtesy), we started the journey home bright and happy. Each of us told his own story on the way. I spoke of everything I had seen and heard in the men's quarters, and she told everything systematically, as in a history, and did not think it right to omit the smallest details.

She was telling everything in order, as if going through a treatise, and when she came to the point at which the medicine was promised, interrupting the narrative she said: "What have we done? How did we forget the promise, the medicine for the eyes?"

I was annoyed at our thoughtlessness and quickly sent one of my men back to ask for the medicine, when the child, who happened to be in her nurse's arms, looked at her mother, and the mother fixing her gaze on the child's eyes, said: "Stop being upset by our carelessness." She said this in a loud voice, joyfully and fearfully. "Nothing of what was promised to us has been omitted, but the true medicine that heals diseases, the cure that comes from prayer, this she has given us, and

it has already worked; nothing at all is left of the disease of the eyes."

As she said this, she took our child and put her in my
arms and I, also, then comprehended the miracles in the
gospel which I had not believed before and I said: "What
a great thing it is for sight to be restored to the blind by
the hand of God, if now His handmaiden makes such
cures and has done such a thing through faith in Him, a
fact no less impressive than these miracles."

This was what he [Sebastopolis] told me, and tears fell
as he spoke and his voice was choked with emotion.
This is the story of the soldier. (*Life of St . Macrina*)

Socrates Scholasticus

Very little is known about the early life of Socrates Scholasticus except that he was born in Constantinople. Virtually nothing is known
about his family and education. Along with other church historians he
continued the practice of recording early Christian history much as Eusebius had done during the preceding century.

Socrates' primary work was titled *Ecclesiastical History,* and it is considered by many scholars to be the most outstanding history of the
church during the fourth and fifth centuries. In many respects it is superior to the historical writings of Eusebius. In collecting information,
Socrates relied heavily on primary sources, including personal interviews
and public documents not previously used in historical research. The author's knowledge was confined almost entirely to the emerging Eastern
church, and he was generally uninformed on the development of the
Christian church in the West.

A major value of Socrates' historical writing to the study of Christian
healing is his account of the influence of spiritual healing in spreading
Christianity into pagan societies on the periphery of the Roman Empire.

The first passages included here are from Socrates' *Ecclesiastical History.* They relate the experience of a Christian woman taken captive
among Iberian people who then inhabited the eastern shore of the Black
Sea in the territory today comprising the republic of Georgia in the So-
viet Union. The name of the captive woman is never given. She is the
second woman in the record of the emerging Eastern Orthodox tradition
to heal disease by spiritual means. She healed two people in this non-
Christian society; both incidents aided in spreading Christianity. This

chapter in Socrates' historical work is titled "In what Manner the Iberians were converted to Christianity."

> ¶ It is now proper to relate how the Iberians about the
> same time became proselytes to the faith. A certain
> woman leading a devout and chaste life, was, in the
> providential ordering of God, taken captive by the
> Iberians. . . . Accordingly the woman in her captivity
> exercised herself among the barbarians in the practice
> of virtue: for she not only maintained the most rigid
> continence, but spent much time in fastings and
> prayers. The barbarians observing this were astonished
> at the strangeness of her conduct.
>
> It happened then that the king's son, then a mere babe,
> was attacked with disease; the queen, according to the
> custom of the country, sent the child to other women
> to be cured, in the hope that their experience would
> supply a remedy. After the infant had been carried
> around by its nurse without obtaining relief from any
> of the women, he was at length brought to this captive.
>
> She had no knowledge of the medical art, and applied
> no material remedy; but taking the child and laying it
> on her bed which was made of horsecloth, in the pres-
> ence of other females, she simply said, 'Christ, who
> healed many, will heal this child also'; then having
> prayed in addition to this expression of faith, and
> called upon God, the boy was immediately restored,
> and continued well from that period.
>
> The report of this miracle spread itself far and wide
> among the barbarian women, and soon reached the
> queen, so that the captive became very celebrated. Not
> long afterwards the queen herself having fallen sick
> sent for the captive woman. Inasmuch as she being a
> person of modest and retiring manners excused herself
> from going, the queen was conveyed to her.
>
> The captive did the same to her as she had done to her
> son before; and immediately the disease was removed.
> And the queen thanked the stranger; but she replied,
> 'this work is not mine, but Christ's, who is the Son of

God that made the world'; she therefore exhorted her to call upon him, and acknowledge the true God.

Amazed at his wife's sudden restoration to health, the king of the Iberians wished to requite with gifts her whom he had understood to be the means of effecting these cures; she however said that she needed not riches, inasmuch as she possessed as riches the consolations of religion; but that she would regard as the greatest present he could offer her, his recognition of the God whom she worshipped and declared. With this she sent back the gifts.

This answer the king treasured up in his mind, and going forth to the chase the next day, the following circumstance occurred: a mist and thick darkness covered the mountain tops and forests where he was hunting, so that their sport was embarrassed, and their path became inextricable. In this perplexity the prince earnestly invoked the gods whom he worshipped; and as it availed nothing, he at last determined to implore the assistance of the captive's God; when scarcely had he begun to pray, ere the darkness arising from the mist was completely dissipated.

Wondering at that which was done, he returned to his palace rejoicing, and related to his wife what had happened; he also immediately sent for the captive stranger, and begged her to inform him who that God was whom she adored. The woman on her arrival caused the king of the Iberians to become a preacher of Christ: for having believed in Christ through this devoted woman, he convened all the Iberians who were under his authority; and when he had declared to them what had taken place in reference to the cure of his wife and child not only, but also the circumstances connected with the chase, he exhorted them to worship the God of the captive.

Thus, therefore, both the king and the queen were made preachers of Christ, the one addressing their male, and other their female subjects. . . . In this way

then, during the days of Constantine, were the Iberians
also converted to Christianity. (Book I, Chap. XX)

The second excerpt from Socrates' writing tells of the healing works
of Christian monks among people on a Mediterranean island which resulted in the establishment of the Christian religion. The title of the
chapter from which this account is extracted is "Assault upon the
Monks, and Banishment of their Superiors, who exhibit Miraculous
Power."

¶ When therefore these wonderful men proved superior to all the violence which was exercised toward
them, Lucius in despair advised the military chief to
send the fathers of the monks into exile: these were
the Egyptian Macarius, and his namesake of Alexandria, both of whom were accordingly banished to an
island where there was no Christian inhabitant, and in
this island there was an idolatrous temple, and a priest
whom the inhabitants worshiped as a god.

On the arrival of these holy men at the island, the
demons of that place were filled with fear and trepi-
dation. Now it happened at the same time that the
priest's daughter became suddenly possessed by a demon, and began to act with great fury, and to overturn
everything that came in her way; nor was any force
sufficient to restrain her, but she cried with a loud
voice to these saints of God, saying: 'Why are ye
come here to cast us out from hence also?'

Then did the men there also display the peculiar
power which they had received through Divine grace:
for having cast out the demon from the maid, and presented her cured to her father, they led the priest himself, and also all the inhabitants of the island to the
Christian faith. Whereupon they immediately brake
their images in pieces, and changed the form of their
temple into that of a church; and having been baptized, they joyfully received instruction in the doctrines of Christianity (Book IV, Chap. XXIV)

The last excerpt from Socrates' *Ecclesiastical History* is a brief account of a Jew suffering from a form of paralysis. This man was healed

and converted to Christianity by baptism. The chapter is titled "A Paralytic Jew healed by Atticus in Baptism."

¶ This was one important improvement in the circumstances of the Church, which happened during the administration of Atticus. Nor were these times without
the attestation of miracles and healings. For a certain
Jew being a paralytic had been confined to his bed for
many years; and as every sort of medical skill, and the
prayers of his Jewish brethren had been resorted to
but had availed nothing, he had recourse at length to
Christian baptism, trusting in it as the only true remedy to be used.

When Atticus the bishop was informed of his wishes,
he instructed him in the first principles of Christian
truth, and having preached to him to hope in Christ,
directed that he should be brought in his bed to the
font. The paralytic Jew receiving baptism with a sin-
cere faith, as soon as he was taken out of the bap-
tismal font found himself perfectly cured of his disease, and continued to enjoy sound health afterwards.

This miraculous power of Christ vouchsafed to be
manifested even in our times; and the fame of it
caused many heathens to believe and be baptized. But
the Jews although zealously 'seeking after signs,' not
even the signs which actually took place were induced to embrace the faith. Such blessings were thus
conferred by Christ upon men. (Book VII, Chap. IV)

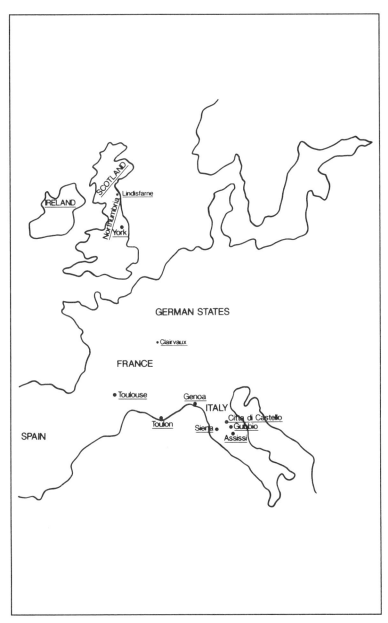

Map 2. A map of northern Europe showing places of recorded Christian healing from the seventh to the fourteenth centuries. The places of healing are underlined.

CHAPTER 6

CUTHBERT AND BEDE

(SEVENTH AND EIGHTH CENTURIES)

Christian healing emerged in northern England during the seventh century, less than one hundred years after an emissary named Augustine (not of Hippo) brought Christianity from Rome. This representative of the Pope became the first Archbishop of Canterbury. He performed impressive healings in his early missionary work.

For several decades a controversy persisted between the followers of early Celtic Christianity and the new form of Christian teachings from Rome. Celtic religious customs placed a much greater emphasis on spiritual healing than did the practices of the Roman medieval church. Yet at a synod in 664 the king of Northumbria and his counselors adopted the Roman form of Christianity. [1]

The conversion of the Britons involved a gradual change from Celtic tribal customs to a more centralized religious rule under the authority of the Vatican. By the end of the seventh century this region experienced a period called "the golden age of Northumbria." Art and literature and religion flourished. It was also the time of two famous English clergymen, Cuthbert and Bede.

Cuthbert (634 – 687) was born in Northumbria and trained in the Celtic monastic tradition. He eventually became the Bishop of Lindisfarne on the northeastern coast of England, yet he lived much of the time on the island of Farne. During a life of consecrated prayer and study of the Bible, he became one of the most notable healers in Christian history.

Cuthbert's life was recorded by two authors. One was an anonymous author and well-educated clergyman who lived at the same time as Cuthbert. [2] The second author was the "Venerable" Bede who lived most of his life after the notable career of Cuthbert. The books by these two authors on the life and works of Cuthbert soon spread throughout England

and to many libraries on the continent. Many churches in England were dedicated to the pious bishop of Lindisfarne. One of the finest cathedrals built in his honor is in the city of Durham. These imposing religious structures are symbols of a great period in England's history. An eminent writer stated:

> However great may have been the artistic, literary, and
> general cultural outlook of the time [of Northumbria],
> it is the great men and women who have left the most
> impressive mark on the history of this period, and of
> these St. Cuthbert rightly takes his place at the very
> forefront. [3]

Relatively little is known about the family and early upbringing of Bede (672 – 735). At the age of seven he received religious training in a monastery at Wearmouth and Jarrow from an abbot named Benedict Biscop. [4] He became a serious student of the Bible and was made a deacon when he was nineteen. He was ordained a priest at the age of thirty. There is no record that Bede ever achieved a higher position in the church. His major role in the history of Christianity is as a biographer of Cuthbert, the famous bishop of his native kingdom. In this role Bede also became a major recorder of Christian healing in the Middle Ages.

Bede's account of the life of Cuthbert was influenced by the earlier biography by an anonymous writer titled *The Life of St. Cuthbert by an Anonymous Author.* This relatively brief work, written between 698 and 705, viewed Cuthbert largely as one of the great clergymen of Northumbria.

Bede acknowledged his indebtedness to the anonymous author (yet never revealed his name) in his biography titled *The Life of St. Cuthbert* (*Vita S. Cuthberti*). This work was more elaborate, refined, and instructive than its predecessor. To Bede, Cuthbert was the universal model of a perfect bishop and church leader. While the anonymous biography explained *how* many events happened in Cuthbert's illustrious life, Bede placed much emphasis on *why* so many good works had happened in the bishop's remarkable career. Benedicta Ward stated:

> For Bede, the question about a saint's miracles was
> not how they happened, but why. The 'how' question
> was already answered: God was acting through all his
> creation, and what provoked wonder was a particu-
> larly interesting message from God that must be ex-
> amined and deciphered. Therefore in rewriting the

>miracles of St. Cuthbert, Bede stresses the meaning to
>be found in them for the reader. [5]

Both biographies describe many incidents of healing. Both were
carefully documented. Much information in both *Lives* was obtained from
personal interviews with individuals who had witnessed Cuthbert's clerical life and were still living when both of the biographies were written.

Bede also wrote another historical classic titled *The Ecclesiastical
History of the English People.* A modern version of this book is titled *A
History of the English Church and People.* It comprises a well-docu-
mented and well-written narrative of religious, political, military, and so-
cial developments in England from the early Roman incursions by Julius
Caesar in 55 B.C. to the reign of King Ethelbald in Northumbria in 731.

Bede was especially careful in his inclusions and descriptions of the
healing works performed by Cuthbert, which have been a subject of
much controversy for many centuries, including our present generation.
In assessing this aspect of Bede's writing, the contemporary English author, Leo Sherley-Price, declared:

>The age of Bede was an age of faith. Almighty God
>was acknowledged as the Source of all life; the world
>was God's world, and Christians were God's people.
>The workings of God were recognized in everyday
>life, and any unusual or striking events, whether
>storms and comets, victories and recoveries of health,
>were regarded as signs of his direct intervention in hu-
>man affairs. God heard and answered prayer, and the
>holiness of his saints enabled them to draw upon the
>hidden powers of the spiritual world in order to work
>wonders and miracles in his Name. [6]

Sherley-Price brings this argument into the twentieth century in additional commentary. He writes:

>In his valuable work *Psychology, Religion, and Heal-
>ing,* Dr. Leslie Weatherhead defines a miracle as 'a
>law-abiding event by which God accomplishes His re-
>demptive purposes through the release of energies
>which belong to a plane of being higher than any with
>which we are normally familiar.' And what we term a
>miracle, whether occurring in the second century or
>the twentieth, may take place as a result of the interac-
>tion of many forces and factors such as faith in God,

the influence of mind over matter, and the power of suggestion. In a miracle a combination of spiritual and mental forces acts upon the material, and modern medicine and psychology are only beginning to recognize the potency of those forces today. God is not bound or restricted in the means by which he manifests his power or answers *the prayer of faith,* and the well-attested miracles that occur today should be a salutary reminder to our materialistic generation that greater things are effected by prayer and faith than we can ever know or comprehend. It is an indication of the temper of the age in which we live that some who profess and call themselves Christians have so little faith in the reality of God's power and mercy that they regard an unmistakable answer to prayer as something unlooked for and extraordinary, almost indecent. It was otherwise among the Christians of Bede's day. [7]

The healing works of Cuthbert as recorded by Bede have had similar long-range influences on members of the modern medical profession. In an article in the *British Medical Journal* (24 – 31 December, 1983), Dr. Rex Gardner explained how the healing miracles described in Bede's historical writings have a significant relevance to new advances in healing disease today. At the time, Dr. Gardner was the President of the Newcastle and Northern Counties Medical Society in England. His article is titled "Miracles of healing in Anglo-Celtic Northumbria as recorded by the Venerable Bede and his contemporaries: a reappraisal in the light of twentieth century experience." (pp. 1927 – 32) Dr. Gardner wrote as follows:

Bede's stories of miracles are seen by some as the chief obstacle to sympathy and rapport with him. Attempts are therefore made to explain them away as due to his different interpretation of history or his view of the function of facts. As well as his need to show Christ to be as powerful as the old pagan lords, it is suggested that we should recognise three men in Bede: the historian, the hagiographer, and the theologian. (p. 1927)

In this article, Dr. Gardner cites seven cases of healing since 1975 in which the use of consecrated prayer at healing services in nearby churches or by supporting relatives, clergy, or friends resulted in complete physical healings, much as similar healings were performed in the time of Cuthbert and Bede. The diseases in these particular cases were verified by physicians as advanced fibrosing alveolitis, Waterhouse-Frid-erichsen syndrome, a central scotoma in one eye, internal bleeding, a fractured pelvis, intra-abdominal hemorrhage, and a large varicose ulcer on one leg. These healings took place in England and Germany as well as in the experiences of Christian missionaries in Nepal and Thailand.

A part of Dr. Gardner's conclusion is as follows:

> A number of case histories of "miraculous" healings in the past 30 years have been presented in which independent corroboration is possible. It is noteworthy that in most cases members of the British medical profession still in practice were actively taking part. No attempt has been made to prove that miracles have occurred, such proof being probably impossible. The adjective "miraculous" is, however, permissible as a convenient shorthand for an otherwise almost inexplicable healing which occurs after prayer to God and brings honour to the Lord Jesus Christ.

> These cases have been paired with miracle stories recorded by Bede and his contemporaries, which up to now have not been considered historically admissible. They have normally been discarded as mere copies of New Testament incidents, or of prototype lives such as that of St. Antony produced to add stature to a local saint. Their writers have been excused as being merely those who put floating tradition into shape or who provided stories which not only delighted the simple minded but filled them with awe and reverence. It is my contention that we can now treat their writings with even greater respect than has up to now been possible. They, and the saint whose lives they portray, prove to be men of greater stature that we have hitherto believed. (p. 1932)

The first readings about the healing works of Cuthbert included below are from *The Life of St. Cuthbert by an Anonymous Author*. The chapter describing this incident is titled "How he healed a woman vexed by a devil." Cuthbert is referred to in several places in this account as the "man of God." The term "prior" refers to his clerical position just below the abbot of a monastery. The first healing is an example of the restoration of health in a situation where the healer is located some distance away from the person who is healed.

¶ There was a certain religious man, specially dear to the man of God, named Hildmer, whose wife was much vexed by a devil. She was greatly ravaged and afflicted to the point of death, grinding her teeth and uttering tearful groans. Now the above-mentioned man, not doubting that she would die a cruel death, set out for our monastery and called St. Cuthbert to him (for at that time he was prior of our church) and explained to him that his wife was sick almost to death.

He did not reveal that she was afflicted with madness, for he was ashamed to declare that a woman once so religious was oppressed by a devil, neither knowing nor understanding that such a trial is wont to fall frequently upon Christians; but he only asked Cuthbert to send a priest with him that she might find peace in the grave.

Now forthwith, the man of God went out to prepare someone to send with him; but hardly had Hildmer departed, when being filled with the Spirit of God, he turned quickly, called him back and said: "It is my duty and not another's, to go with you." Then the man of God prepared himself and they all rode together on horseback; his companion was weeping and mourning for two reasons, because his wife was dying and he was bereaved and his children left desolate, and more especially because of the disgraceful insane condition in which he knew that she was about to be seen by the man of God, whereby she was horribly degraded and shamelessly destroyed and polluted with spittle, she who had once been so modest and chaste.

Knowing this the man of God began to console him with kindly words and revealed fully the nature of her infirmity, which the husband had hidden from him, and finally added with prophetic words: "Now when we come to your house, your wife whom you believe to be dead will come to meet me and on receiving this horse's reins which I hold in my hand, will, though the help of God, be restored to full health and will minister to us, and the demon will be driven away."

So they came to the homestead, as we have said, the man of God (and his friends); the woman, as if rising from sleep, came to meet them and at first touch of the reins, the demon was completely driven away, and, as she thankfully declared, she was restored to her former health and ministered to them. (Book II, Chap. VIII)

The following chapters from the *Anonymous Life* relate the healings of the wife of a gesith (a well-born companion or the attendant of an Anglo-Saxon king), a maiden, a paralytic boy, an infant child, and a servant of a gesith. In these accounts, Cuthbert is referred to as the "holy bishop." The healing of the paralytic boy and the servant reveals an attachment to the Old Testament belief that a person suffering from a physical disease is being punished by God for his sins. The healing of the infant child shows the power of God capable of destroying disease caused by a plague.

¶ Among these miracles there is the case of Hemma a certain gesith, dwelling in the district called *Kintis,* whose wife was almost at the point of death through her infirmity. As our holy bishop was preaching the word of God to the people, he came to the village of the above-mentioned gesith, who immediately went out to meet the bishop, and, thanking the Lord for his coming, received him and his company with kindness and ministered to them; after washing their hands and feet, he revealed to the holy bishop the sorrow and grief of all his family, namely that his wife's life was despaired of even as if she were already dead.

He prayed him to bless some water, believing that by means of it, if she had been appointed to die, she would die more easily, or if life were given back she would be healed more quickly. The holy bishop sat down and blessed the water in front of them all and gave it to his priest named Beta who still lives. He took it and carried it to her chamber where, like a dead woman, she lay breathing her last. He sprinkled it over her and the bed and, opening her mouth, she tasted some of the water.

She at once recovered her senses and blessed God who had sent her such guests to restore her to health. And forthwith, rising up healed, like Peter's wife's mother, she ministered to them. (Book IV, Chap. III)

¶ I learned from the personal account of the priest Aethilwald who is now prior of the monastery which is called Melrose, how another infirmity and sickness was healed when he himself was present. For he said: "On a certain day we came with the holy bishop to a village which is called *Bedesfeld*. Now there a certain maiden, a relation and kinswoman of mine, was ill; for she had suffered great pain in her head and in the whole of one side for the space of nearly a year, and no doctor could heal her with any poulticing of the body. And so our bishop, hearing of the illness with which the maiden was afflicted, on our request took pity on her, anointing her with chrism [an ointment] consecrated by his blessing, and she quickly recovered strength from that hour; the pain left her gradually from day to day, and she was restored to her former health." (Book IV, Chap. IV)

¶ There is also another similar miracle which I have plainly learned about from the account of many reliable men who were present, one of whom is Penna, who said: "At a certain time the holy bishop was making his way from Hexham to the city which is called Carlisle. Nevertheless a halt was made in the middle of the journey in a district which is called *Ahse*. For when the people had gathered together from the mountains, he placed his hand on the head of each of them, and anointing them with consecrated oil he blessed them, and remained there two days preaching the word of God.

"Meanwhile there came some women bearing a certain youth who lay on a litter; they carried him to the wood not far from our tents where the holy bishop was, and sent a messenger asking and adjuring him in the name of our Lord Jesus Christ that he would bless him with his holy relics and would utter a prayer for him to the Lord, beseeching God's pardon for the sins by which he was bound and on account of which he endured punishment.

"So the bishop, seeing their unwavering faith, put us forth from him and prayed to the Lord, and, blessing the boy, he drove away the disease and restored him to health. For the boy arose that very hour and took food, and departed with the women, thanking and magnifying the Lord who had wrought wonderful things in His servants." (Book IV, Chap. V)

¶ I consider that I ought not to pass over in silence a work of mercy which a priest of our monastery described as happening in his presence; he is still alive, but he was then a layman and the servant of a certain gesith. He says: "Now at that time when the holy bishop set out to preach the word of God among the common people, he was invited by my master Sibba, a gesith of King Ecgfrith, who lived near the river called the Tweed, and came to his village with a company of people piously singing psalms and hymns.

"My master received him kindly and told him of a servant of his who was wretchedly afflicted with infirmity and whose life was despaired of and who was even now dying and breathing his last. The holy bishop had pity on him and blessing some water bade me administer it to him, saying: 'Give the water to your lord's sick servant, with the help of God, according to our faith which brings salvation, and may the Lord pardon him for sins for which he is afflicted; and either in this present world, if he is to live, or in the world to come, if he is to die, may he grant him rest from his labour.'

"I forthwith obeyed his command and thrice I gave him to drink and without delay (for the Holy Spirit knows nothing of tardy endeavours), I beheld him brought back to life and restored to his former health by the help of the Spirit of God. He is still alive and giving

thanks to the Lord and blessing the bishop, for whom
he has never ceased to pray." (Book IV, Chap. VII)

The next set of excerpts is from *The Life of St. Cuthbert by Bede*. The
first incident is a healing of Cuthbert himself by some of the brethren at
his monastery. His disease was caused by a plague which extended over
the entire territory of Britain. Physical complications remained on Cuthbert's body for some time after a significant but partial healing. Like the
Apostle Paul who had a "thorn in the flesh," Cuthbert evidently continued to pray for a complete healing and used the discomfort as a challenge
to rely more effectively on God. Other narratives tell of the healing of a
girl, a sick man, and two young men who were dying.

¶ At that time (as Herefrith, a priest who belonged to
his community and who was once abbot of the
monastery of Lindisfarne, testifies that Cuthbert was
wont to relate), he was stricken down with the plague
which at that time carried off very many throughout
the length and breadth of Britain.

Now the brethren of that monastery spent the whole
night in watching and praying for his life and safety;
for they all thought that inasmuch as he was a holy
man, his continued presence in the flesh was necessary
to them. When one of them told him about this in the
morning — for they had done it without his knowledge — he replied forthwith: "And why do I lie here?
for doubtless God has not despised the prayers of so
many good men. Give me my staff and shoes."

And immediately he arose and began to try to walk,
leaning upon his staff; and as his strength grew from
day to day, he recovered his health; but as the swelling
which appeared on his thigh gradually left the surface
of his body, it sank into the inward parts and, throughout almost the whole of his life, he continued to feel
some inward pains, so that, in the words of the apostle,
"strength was made perfect in weakness." (Chap. VIII)

¶ There are many who have borne witness to a miracle
of healing wrought in their presence by the venerable
Bishop Cuthbert not unlike this last one; among these
witnesses is the pious priest Aethilwald, then a servant

of the man of God, but now the abbot of the monastery at Melrose. For while according to his custom he was going through all the villages teaching, he came to a certain village in which there were a few nuns to whom he, the man of God, had a short time before given a place of abode in that village, when they had fled from their own monastery through fear of the barbarian army.

One of these, a kinswoman of the same priest Aethilwald, was afflicted by a very severe illness; for all through the year she had been troubled with an intolerable pain in the head and in the whole of one side, and had been entirely given up by the physicians. When those who had come with him told the man of God about her and prayed for her restoration, he had pity on her and anointed the wretched woman with holy oil. She began to get better from that very hour and after a few days was restored to complete health. (Chap. XXX)

¶ Nor do we consider that we ought to pass over in silence a miracle which, as we have learned, was performed by the virtue of the same venerable man, though he himself was absent. We have already mentioned the reeve [a local administrative official of the king] Hildmer whose wife the man of God freed from an unclean spirit.

Now this same reeve afterwards took to his bed with a most serious illness, and, as his affliction grew from day to day, he seemed already to be at the point of death. Many of his friends came to console the afflicted man. And as they sat by the bed in which he lay, suddenly one of them recalled that he had some bread with him, which Cuthbert, the man of the Lord, had recently blessed and given to him. "And I believe", he said, "that Hildmer by tasting this can receive healing, if only the slowness of our faith does not hinder."

Now they were all laymen, but devout. So turning to each other, they confess one by one that they believed without any doubt that he could be healed by partaking of this blessed bread. They filled a cup with water and put in a very little of the bread, and gave it to him to drink.

No sooner had the draught of water, sanctified by the bread, reached his stomach, than all the inward pain disappeared as well as the outward wasting of his limbs. His health returned without delay, and brought strength back to the man who had thus been set free from affliction, deservedly stirring him and all who saw or heard of the swiftness of so unexpected a cure, to praise the holiness of the servant of God and to wonder at the power of true faith. (Chap. XXXI)

¶ Once too, as the most holy shepherd of the Lord's flock was going round visiting his sheepfields, he came to mountainous and wild regions where there were many gathered together from the widely scattered villages, on whom he was to lay his hands. But in the mountains no church could be found, nor any place fit to receive the bishop and his retinue. So they pitched tents for him by the wayside and, cutting down branches from the neighbouring wood, they made every man for himself booths to dwell in as best they could.

There the man of God had been preaching the word for two days to the crowds who flocked to hear him, and by the laying on of hands had ministered the grace of the Holy Spirit to those who had lately been regenerated in Christ, when suddenly there appeared some women bearing upon a pallet a youth, wasted with a long and grievous sickness. Placing him on the edge of the wood, they sent to the bishop, praying that he would allow him to be brought to him to receive his blessing.

When the youth had been brought to Cuthbert and he saw his terrible affliction, he bade them all go farther off. And turning to his wonted weapon of prayer, he gave his blessing and drove away the plague which the careful hands of the doctors could not expel with their

compounds and drugs. Thereupon the youth rose up
the same hour, received food and was strengthened
and, giving thanks to God, he returned to the women
who had carried him. And so it came to pass that he
returned home well and joyful, amid the rejoicings of
the same women who had sorrowfully conveyed him
thither when he was sick. (Chap. XXXII)

¶ At the same time there suddenly arose in those parts a
most grievous pestilence, and brought with it destruc-
tion so severe that in some large villages and estates
once crowded with inhabitants, only a small and scattered remnant, and sometimes none at all, remained.

So the most holy father Cuthbert, diligently traversing
his diocese, did not cease to bring the ministry of the
word and the help of much-needed consolation to the
poor few who remained. Coming to one village and
having helped by his exhortations all whom he found,
he said to his priest: "Do you think that anyone is left
in these parts who needs to be visited and exhorted by
us; or have we seen all who are in trouble and can we
now pass on to others?"

The priest, looking round everywhere, saw a woman
standing at a distance who, having lost one son a little
while before, was now holding his brother in her arms
at the point of death; her eyes, streaming with tears,
bore witness both to her past and her present troubles.
The priest pointed her out to the man of God, who did
not delay but, approaching her and giving her his
blessing, kissed the boy and said to the mother: "Do
not fear nor be sad; for your infant will be healed and
will live, nor will anyone else be missing from your
home through this plague." The mother herself and her
son lived along afterwards to bear testimony to the
truth of this prophecy. (Chap. XXXIII)

The final set of excerpts is from Bede's *History of the English Church
and People*. This book contains numerous accounts of healings performed by several prominent clergymen in addition to a chapter about
the life and works of Cuthbert.

The first excerpts relate healings performed by Germanus, a bishop who visited England from the continent.

> ¶ A man who held the status of a tribune came forward with his wife and asked the bishops to cure his blind daughter, a child of ten. They directed him to take her to their opponents, but the latter, smitten by guilty consciences, joined their entreaties to those of the girl's parents and begged the bishops to heal her.
>
> Seeing their opponents yield, they offered a short prayer; then Germanus, being filled with the Holy Ghost, called on the Trinity, and taking into his hands a casket containing relics of the saints that hung around his neck, he applied to the girl's eyes in the sight of them all.
>
> To the joy of the parents and the amazement of the crowd, the child's sight was emptied of darkness and filled with the light of truth. Thenceforward all erroneous arguments were expunged from the minds of the people, who eagerly accepted the teaching of the bishops. (Book I, Chap. 18)
>
> ¶ Meanwhile evil spirits throughout the land had been reluctantly compelled to foretell Germanus' coming, so that a local chieftain named Elaphius hurried to meet the saints before receiving any definite news. He brought with him his son, who in the very flower of his youth was crippled by a painful disease of the leg, whose muscles had so contracted that the limb was entirely useless. . .
>
> Suddenly Elaphius threw himself at the bishops' feet, and presented to them his son, the sight of whose infirmity proclaimed his need louder than words. All were moved to pity at the spectacle, especially the bishops, who earnestly prayed God to show mercy.
>
> Blessed Germanus then asked the youth to sit down, and drawing out the leg bent with disease, he passed his healing hand over the afflicted area, and at his touch health was swiftly returned. The withered limb

filled, the muscles regained their power, and in the
presence of them all the lad was restored healed to his
parents. . . .Henceforward, the Faith was maintained
uncorrupted in Britain for a long time. (Book I, Chap.
21)

The next passages describe a healing done by Augustine, the first
Archbishop of Canterbury.

¶ Meanwhile, with the aid of King Ethelbert, Augustine summoned the bishops and teachers of the nearest
British province to a conference at a place still known
to the English as Augustine's Oak, which lies on the
border between the Hwiccas and the West Saxons. He
began by urging them to establish brotherly relations
with him in Catholic unity, and to join with him in
God's work of preaching the gospel to the heathen. . . .

Augustine then brought this lengthy and fruitless conference to a close, saying: 'Let us ask our Lord, *who
makes men to be of one mind* in His Father's house, to
grant us a sign from heaven and show us which tradition is to be followed, and by what roads we are to
hasten our steps towards His kingdom. Bring in some
sick person, and let the beliefs and practice of those
who can heal him be accepted as pleasing to God and
to be followed by all.'

On the reluctant agreement of his opponents, a blind
Englishman was led in and presented to the British
priests, from whose ministry he obtained no healing or
benefit. Then Augustine, as the occasion demanded,
knelt in prayer to the Father of our Lord Jesus Christ,
imploring that the man's lost sight might be restored
and prove the means of bringing the light of spiritual
grace to the minds of countless believers. Immediately
the blind man's sight was restored, and all acknowledged Augustine as the true herald of the light of
Christ. (Book II, Chap. 2)

The last group of excerpts relates healings done by John of Beverly, a
famous bishop of Hexham and York.

¶ At the beginning of King Aldfrid's reign Bishop Eata died, and was succeeded as Bishop of Hexham by a holy man named John [of Beverly]. Many miracles are told of him by those who knew him well, and in particular by Berthun, a most reverend and truthful man, formerly John's deacon and now abbot of the monastery known as In-Derawuda, which means 'In the wood of Deiri'. I have thought it fitting to preserve the memory of some of these.

Whenever opportunity offered and especially during Lent, this man of God used to retire with a few companions to read and pray quietly in an isolated house surrounded by open woodland and a dyke. It stood about a mile and a half from the church at Hexham across the river Tyne, and had a burial-ground dedicated to Saint Michael the Archangel. John once came to stay here at the beginning of Lent and, as was his invariable custom, told his companions to find some poor person who was either seriously infirm or in dire want, so that he might live with them during their stay and benefit from their alms.

In a village not far distant lived a dumb youth known to the bishop; for he had often visited him to receive alms and had never been able to utter a single word. In addition, he had so many scabs and scales on his head that no hair ever grew on the crown, but only a few wisps stood up in a ragged circle round it. So the bishop ordered this youth to be fetched, and a little hut to be made for him in the enclosure round the house where he could live and receive his daily allowance.

When one week of Lent was past, on the following Sunday John told the poor lad to come to him, and when he had entered he ordered him to put out his tongue and show it to him; then he took him by the chin, and making the sign of the holy cross on his tongue, told him to retract it and speak.

'Pronounce some word,' he said: 'say *yea,*' which is the English word of agreement and assent, i. e. 'Yes'. The lad's tongue was loosed, and at once he did what he was told. The bishop then proceeding to the names of letters: 'Say A.' And he said 'A'. 'Now say B,' he said, which the youth did. And when he had repeated the names of each of the letters after the bishop, the latter added syllables and words for him to repeat after him. When he had uttered every word accordingly, the bishop set him to repeat longer sentences, and he did so.

All those who were present say that all day and the next night, as long as he could keep awake, the youth never stopped saying something and expressing his own inner thoughts and wishes to others, which he had never been able to do previously. He was like the cripple healed by the Apostles Peter and John, who stood up, leaped, and walked, entering the temple with them, *walking, and leaping, and praising God,* rejoicing in the use of his feet, of which he had been so long deprived.

The bishop was delighted at his cure, and directed the physician to undertake the cure of the youth's scabby head. The physician did as he was asked, and with the assistance of the bishop's blessing and prayers his skin healed, and a vigorous growth of hair appeared. So the youth obtained a clear complexion, readiness of speech, and a beautiful head of hair, whereas he had formerly been deformed, destitute, and dumb. In his joy at this recovery, he declined an offer from the bishop of a permanent place in his household, preferring to return to his own home. (Book V, Chap. 2)

¶ Berthun described another miracle done by the bishop. When the most reverend Wilfrid became Bishop of Hexham after his long exile, and John became Bishop of York on the death of the holy and humble Bosa, he came one day to a convent of nuns at a place called Wetadun, ruled at the time by the Abbess Heriburg.

When we had arrived and been welcomed with general rejoicing, the abbess informed us that one of the nuns, her own daughter, was very seriously ill. She told us that the nun had recently been bled in the arm and that, while she was being treated, she was suddenly seized by a violent pain which rapidly increased, so that the wounded arm grew worse and became so swollen that it could hardly be encircled with two hands. In consequence, the nun was lying in bed in terrible pain and seemed likely to die.

The abbess therefore begged the bishop to visit her and give her his blessing, being sure that she would improve if the bishop blessed or touched her. . . . So he went in, taking me with him to see the girl who, as I have said, lay helpless and in great pain, with her arm swollen to such a size that she could not bend her elbow.

The bishop stood and said a prayer over her, and having given her blessing, went out. Some while later, as we were sitting at table, someone came in and asked me to come outside, saying: "Coenburg" — for that was the girl's name — "wishes you to come back to her room at once."

I did so, and when I entered, I found her looking cheerful and apparently in sound health. And when I sat down by her, she said: "Would you like me to ask for a drink?" "Certainly," I replied, "I shall be delighted if you will." When a cup had been brought and we had both drunk, she began to tell me what had happened.

"As soon as the bishop had blessed me and gone away, I began to feel better; and although I have not yet recovered my full strength, the pain has entirely left my arm where it was most intense, and all my body. It was as though the bishop took it away with him entirely when he left, although the swelling on my arm seems to remain."

As we were leaving the convent, the disappearance of the pain in her limbs was promptly followed by a subsidence of the swelling, and the girl, saved from pain and death, gave thanks to our Lord and Saviour with all the other servants of God in the place. (Book V, Chap. 3)

¶ I cannot leave unmentioned a miracle that God's servant Heribald relates as having been performed for his benefit by Bishop John. At the time he was one of the bishop's clergy, but is now abbot of a monastery near the mouth of the river Tyne.

'Living with him, and knowing his way of life very intimately,' he says, 'I knew it to be wholly worthy of a bishop, so far as it is permissible for a man to judge. But I also proved by the experience of many others, and more especially by my own, how great his merit was in the eyes of him who sees the heart; for by his prayer and blessing, as I shall tell, he brought me back from death's door and restored me to life.

In my early youth I lived among his clergy, occupied in learning to read and sing; but my heart had not yet entirely abandoned youthful follies. As we were travelling with him one day, we happened to come to a level road, well suited for galloping our horses.

The young men with him, mainly layfolk, began to ask the bishop's permission to gallop and try out their horses against each other. At first he refused their request, saying that it was an unprofitable occupation; but at length he gave in to their unanimous wish, saying: "Do so if you wish; but Heribald is not to take part in the race." I begged him persistently to let me race with the rest, for I had confidence in an excellent horse he had given me; but I could not obtain his consent.

When they had galloped to and fro several times, and came back spurring their horses in a race while the bishop and I watched, my hot-headed willfulness got the better of me, and I could not restrain myself. Despite his prohibition, I joined in the sport and began to race with the others at full speed. As I did so, I heard the bishop behind me saying in a sorrowful voice: "Oh, how you grieve me by riding like that!" But, although I heard him, I went on against his orders.

Shortly afterwards, as my spirited horse took off in a powerful jump across a hollow in the path, I fell, and at once lost all feeling and power of movement as though I were dying; for at the spot lay a stone, level with the ground, lightly covered by turf, the only stone to be found in the whole of that level plain. And it happened by chance, or rather by the disobedience of divine providence as a punishment for my disobedience, that I struck my head, and the hand which I had put under my head as I fell, on this stone. As a consequence, my thumb was broken and my skull cracked, and, as I said, I lay as though dead.

As I was unable to move, they stretched an awning over me for protection; and from an hour after midday until evening I lay motionless as a corpse. Then I revived slightly, and my companions carried me home, where I lay speechless all night, vomiting blood as a result of some internal injury.

The bishop was greatly distressed about my accident and possible death, because he was especially fond of me; and he did not remain with his clergy that night as was his usual custom, but spent all night in vigil and prayer, as I understand, asking God of His mercy to restore me to health.

Early next morning he came and said a prayer over me, calling me by name, and waking me out of what seemed to be a heavy sleep. "Do you know who is speaking to you?" he asked. Opening my eyes, I replied: "I do. You are my beloved bishop." "Can you live?" he asked. "I can do so with the help of your prayers, God willing," I replied.

Having laid his hand on my head and blessed me, he went back to his prayers. On his return after a short while, he found me sitting up and well enough to talk. Then, inspired by God — as was soon evident — he asked me if I knew for certain whether I had been baptized. . . .

He then proceeded to catechize me on the spot; and when he happened to breathe on my face, I immediately began to feel better. He called the surgeon, and told him to close and bandage up the crack in my

skull. After receiving his blessing, I was so much better next day that I mounted my horse and journeyed on
with him to another town. I was soon completely recovered, and was then cleansed in the lifegiving waters of Baptism. (Book V, Chap. 6)

CHAPTER 7

BERNARD OF CLAIRVAUX
AND MALACHY

(ELEVENTH AND TWELFTH CENTURIES)

Bernard of Clairvaux (1091 – 1153) had a unique influence on the evolution of Christianity and Christian healing during the late Middle Ages. In some respects the life of this unusual clergyman was as diversified as that of Augustine. He did not exert the widespread impact on Christian theology by voluminous and elaborate writings as the famous bishop of Hippo, but he promoted a variety of church reforms as a persuasive and ardent activist. He was also one of the most effective healers of the Middle Ages.

Bernard was born near Dijon in central France into a family of the Burgundian nobility. Because he was a timid and unassuming youth, his parents prepared him for a clerical career. At first he showed few qualifications for leadership in the church. Yet when he entered a monastic order at Citeaux in 1113, he achieved the astonishing feat of persuading some thirty friends and relatives to join him in the rigors of monastic life.

Bernard used this newly-discovered ability to arouse deep religious feelings in skeptical listeners for the remainder of his life. It helped make him one of the major leaders of the Middle Ages. It also helped him in healing the sick. Bokenkotter declared: "As preacher, author, and guide of souls, he was the chief force behind the spiritual revival of the twelfth century as well as being one of the most illustrious statesmen of the time." [1]

Bernard joined the Cistercian order and founded a new monastic center at Clairvaux in 1115. From this base his clerical order spread its spiritual vitality to Italy, Germany, England, Spain, and Ireland. By 1300 the Cistercians had almost 700 monasteries scattered throughout Europe. [2] Bernard was also influential in the affairs of the medieval church far be-

yond the confines of Clairvaux. He was instrumental in the selection of a
pope in 1145, a feat that strengthened his reputation as "the uncrowned
emperor of Europe." [3] He was a severe critic of Scholasticism with its
emphasis on rationalism and the secular orientation of Aristotle. He was
a chief spokesman for the Second Crusade to recapture Jerusalem from
Moslem rule, a venture which ended in total failure and a large loss of
life.

Much of our knowledge of Bernard's healing works comes from accounts about his life written by numerous contemporary authors and later
biographers. From this literature, the founder of the monastery at Clairvaux emerges as an active and gifted healer. Many of his healings were
intermixed with symbols and rituals of the church in the High Middle
Ages. These methods included the use of the sign of a cross, baptism, the
eucharist, and confession. Bernard's healings also involved the use of
prayer.

A biography of Bernard written by M. Theodore Ratisborne in 1843
related one of Bernard's healings as follows:

> The cures were so many that the witnesses themselves
> were unable to detail them all. At Donigen, near Rhe-
> infeld, where the first Sunday of Advent was spent,
> Bernard cured, in one day, nine blind people, ten who
> were deaf or dumb, and eighteen lame or paralytic. On
> the following Wednesday, at Schaffhausen, the num-
> ber of miracles increased. . . .[4]

Another biography by J. Cotter Morison in 1868 describes a healing
experience of Bernard as follows:

> Thirty-six miraculous cures in one day would seem to
> have been the largest stretch of supernatural power
> which Bernard permitted to himself. The halt, the
> blind, the deaf, and the dumb were brought from all
> parts to be touched by Bernard. The patient was pre-
> sented to him, whereupon he made the sign of the
> cross over the part affected, and the cure was perfect. [5]

The following incident was related in Morison's book from the writings of one of Bernard's companions.

> ¶ At Toulouse, in the church of St. Saturninus, in
> which we were lodged, was a certain regular canon,
> named John. John had kept his bed for seven months,

and was so reduced that his death was expected daily. His legs were so shrunken that they were scarcely larger than a child's arms. He was quite unable to rise to satisfy the wants of nature. At last his brother canons refused to tolerate his presence any longer among them, and thrust him out into the neighboring village.

When the poor creature heard of Bernard's proximity, he implored to be taken to him. Six men, therefore, carrying him as he lay in bed, brought him into a room close to that in which we were lodged. The abbot heard him confess his sins, and listened to his entreaties to be restored to health.

Bernard mentally prayed to God: "Behold, O Lord, they seek for a sign, and our words avail nothing, unless they be confirmed with signs following." He then blessed him and left the chamber, and so did we all. In that very hour the sick man arose from his couch. . . . [6]

A graphic account of some of Bernard's healing work is included in a book by Bruno S. James titled *Saint Bernard of Clairvaux: An Essay in Biography,* published in 1957. The first passages excerpted from this book relate some of the problems Bernard had with members of his own family who had joined him in the monastery at Clairvaux, but were somewhat envious and concerned about his fame as a popular healer. The second incident shows a deep sense of love (and humor) in Bernard's mind that facilitated the process of healing. It also explains that Bernard himself suffered at times from ill health. The second healing reveals a trace of the Old Testament belief that sickness is inflicted by God to punish man for his sins.

¶ The miracles of Bernard were hardly less embarrassing to himself and his community than they are to some of us. His uncle Gaudry seems to have been highly suspicious of them. More than once he nearly reduced Bernard to tears by telling him that for a man like him to attempt to do miracles was sheer presumption, and that at any rate there was nothing in them.

But one day Gaudry himself fell seriously ill and at once sent for Bernard and begged him to bless and cure him. "Sorry, my dear Uncle," said Bernard smiling, "I fear I can't do that, it would be sheer presumption for me to attempt any such thing." Whereupon Gaudry pleaded that he had only been trying to save his nephew from pride, that he had not really meant what he had said about his miracles.

In the end Bernard blessed him and cured him both of his illness and of scoffing at his miracles.[7]

¶ On another occasion William of St. Theirry fell ill and Bernard, who was none too well himself at the time, sent him a message by his brother Gerard asking him to come to Clairvaux to keep him company and promising that he would either get quite well there or die. The good William tells us that he was both delighted and flattered by the invitation and could hardly make up his mind whether it would be better to live or to die in that holy man's company. He gives us a charming picture of himself and Bernard, both sick men, chatting together of spiritual things in the infirmary or whatever did service as an infirmary at Clairvaux.

William recovered from his illness and by the Saturday before Septuagesima his health was so far restored that, although still a little weak, he began to think it was time for him to return to his monastery. However Bernard would not hear of his leaving Clairvaux just yet. He persuaded him to stay on until the beginning of Lent and one feels that he did not have much difficulty in doing so. But William insisted that if he was to stay on he should at least begin again to abstain from meat. Bernard was strongly opposed to this and William stubbornly determined on it.

And so they parted for the night, William to his bed and Bernard to Compline. They had obviously quarrelled as even holy men will. That night poor William's illness returned worse than ever. He was seized with the most excruciating pains and as he tossed and turned on his bed he began to wonder if he would ever live to see the dawn and talk to Bernard again.

But dawn came at last and with the dawn came Bernard looking rather severe. "Well," he said, "what will you have to eat now?" Then poor William realized that his illness had returned in order to punish him for his obstinacy of the night before and meekly replied that he would eat whatever he was given.

Whereupon Bernard broke into one of his gay laughs and assured him that he would not die and that he would send up for him a good helping of meat. "And," says William, "I became immediately as well as ever except for feeling a little weak owing to my sleepless night." [8]

One of the most thorough accounts of the healing works of Bernard is contained in Benedicta Ward's book, *Miracles and the Medieval Mind,* published in 1982. Bernard's use of healing works, Ward explains, was to exemplify "signs of the power of God" in order to emphasize Christian virtues and to bring non-believers into the ranks of the Christian church. [9] Ward discusses in considerable detail the extensive biography of Bernard written by three of his contemporaries, titled *Vita Prima Bernardi*. This work included numerous healings by the famous leader of the monastery at Clairvaux. The three men traveled with Bernard and witnessed his healing works. One of them (Geoffrey of Auxere) had been Bernard's secretary.

During a visit with Bernard to Germany in 1146 – 1147, the three companions compiled a daily record of some of his healings. They were assisted by selected persons who contributed their own observations. One of these accounts included the following commentary:

> *Eberhard:* On that day I saw him cure three others who were lame.
> *Franco:* You all saw the blind woman who came into church and received her sight before the people.
> *Guadricus:* and a girl whose hand was withered had it healed, while the chant at the offertory was being sung.
> *Gerard:* on the same day I saw a boy receive his sight. [10]

The complete record of Bernard's brief tour in Germany states that he performed 235 healings among crippled people, 172 healings of blind people, and numerous other healings of persons who had been deaf, dumb, and demon-possessed. Ward's coverage of the *Vita Prima* also relates how Bernard healed numerous people of all kinds of diseases in Milan and in various regions of France.

The first group of the following readings is from *St. Bernard of Clairvaux,* which is a portion of the *Vita Prima Bernardi.* The chapter containing these descriptions is titled "His Miracles of Healing." The first incident involves the healing of a nobleman who was a relative of Bernard and had opposed the church. He had also mistreated the poor and less fortunate people in his province. The healing included a promise to cease sinning and to uphold Christian teachings and morality.

> ¶ I shall tell you now of the first miracles which Christ worked through His servant Bernard for all the world to see. When he had been at Clairvaux for some years, it happened that a certain nobleman, who was also a relative of his, fell grievously ill.
>
> The name of this man was Josbert de la Ferte, and his lands were quite near the monastery. The illness came upon him very suddenly, and caused him to lose the power of speech, and to go out of his mind. His son, Josbert the Younger, and his many friends, were smitten with grief at this misfortune, especially because such an honoured and important personage looked like dying without the chance to confess his sins and receive Holy Viaticum.
>
> Bernard was away from the monastery, and so a messenger was sent to him post-haste. The abbot arrived three days after the disaster, and found him lying on his bed of pain. The pitiful state of the man and the grief of the son and friends were so moving that the saint put all his trust in God's mercy, and spoke to those around in these words: 'You all know that this man has laid a heavy hand upon the Church in these parts, and you cannot fail to realize how he has tyrannized the poor and sinned against God. You must give me your word, then, that what he has stolen will be returned to the rightful owners, and that the rights of which he has deprived the poor will be restored. You must promise me that he will confess his sins and then receive the sacraments.'

Everyone was struck with wonder at these words, for the promise of Josbert's return to health filled the son and the whole household with great joy. Everything that Bernard had told them to do, they promised to do, and did.

But the saint's brother, Gerard, and his uncle Gaudry, were very upset and frightened by his promise, and unknown to the rest of the community they came to him to reprove him for it with harsh criticism. However, Bernard's reply to them was straightforward and to the point. 'God can easily do what you find hard to credit.' And then, after a short prayer, the abbot went to say Mass.

He had not had time to finish before a messenger arrived with the news that Josbert's speech had been completely restored, and that he was asking Bernard to come quickly to him. When Bernard had finished Mass, he hurried to his bedside, and Josbert contritely confessed his sins with many tears and received the sacraments.

Now that his life had been saved and he could speak again, the nobleman set about fulfilling Bernard's commands without any wavering or excuse: he even disposed of many of his possessions and gave alms with the proceeds. (Chap. XVI, para. 1, 2)

The next brief account tells of Bernard healing a young child of a deformed arm and hand.

¶ One day Bernard was returning from work in the fields when he met a poor woman who had come from afar to bring to the saint her child whose hand had been withered and whose arm had been twisted and deformed from birth.

The saint was so moved by the mother's entreaties that he told her to set the child down while he prayed and made the sign of the Cross over it and especially over its hand and arm. He then told the mother to call her child to come to her, and it ran and embraced her with

both arms. From that moment the deformity disappeared and the child began to enjoy perfect health.
(Chap. XVI, para. 3)

The following excerpt relates another healing of a youth by Bernard. It
is taken from a chapter titled "Miracles Worked Among His Monks."

¶ Godfrey, the Bishop of Langres, who was a relative
of Bernard's, and who had entered the monastic life
with him and become his inseparable friend, used to
tell the story of how Guy [a relative of Bernard's] had
been present at the first miracle he saw him perform.

They were passing through Chateau-Landon, in the
territory of the Seine, when a young man who had a
fistula on his foot begged and entreated the saint to
touch the spot and bless it. Bernard made the sign of
the Cross over the infected part, and at once it began
to clear.

A few days later, on their journey back through the
town, Bernard and his companions found the young-
ster in perfect health, with no trace of the fistula.
(Chap. XVII, para. 7)

Bernard was one of the very few Christian leaders in the Middle Ages
who performed many physical and mental healings and at the same time
recorded in written form his ideas and observations about Christian healing. His major writing of this kind was *The Life and Death of Saint
Malachy The Irishman.* Bernard's own life was the subject matter of numerous biographies by contemporary and later authors; he was also a biographer himself writing about another Christian clergyman who performed many healing works.

Malachy (1094 – 1148) was born in Armagh, Ireland, into a pagan
family. He became a Christian in his youth, and was ordained a priest at
the age of twenty-five. He began performing healings and did other notable services for the church that aided him in gaining appointment as the
Bishop of Connor and Down. Several years thereafter Malachy lived for
a time in a monastic retreat. His reputation as a church leader gradually
spread throughout Ireland. He was eventually appointed as the Archbishop of Armagh in his native province.

In 1139 Malachy traveled to Rome, where he was appointed by the
pope as the papal legate in Ireland. On his return, Malachy visited Clair-

vaux and began a life-long friendship with Bernard. He introduced the
Cistercian monastic practices to Ireland on his return. He also continued
to perform many healings.

Malachy made a second visit to Rome in 1148 and returned again to
Clairvaux. Here he died in the presence of Bernard. His life and works
had greatly impressed Bernard, who undertook the writing of the life of
this unusual Christian leader. Bernard relied on Malachy's assistants and
co-workers in Ireland for information for this biographical work.

The last group of readings in this chapter is from Bernard's biography,
The Life and Death of Saint Malachy the Irishman. Twelve healings are
related in this book. Only a few of these incidents are described here.
One account tells of protection from an injury. The others are healings of
physical disease.

> ¶ Then at Father Imar's command he [Malachy] took
> with him about ten of the brethren and, arriving at the
> place, began to build. It happened one day while he
> was cutting with an axe that one of the workmen acci-
> dentally got in his way while he was raising the axe
> and it fell on his spine with full force. He fell to the
> ground and everyone rushed up, thinking he was mor-
> tally wounded or dead. His tunic was rent from top to
> bottom.
>
> But the man was found unharmed, his skin so slightly
> wounded that only a slight scratch appeared on its sur-
> face. The man whom the axe had laid out stood up un-
> scathed in the sight and to the amazement of those
> standing around. Because of this they became more
> eager and from then on were found more ready for
> work. This was the beginning of the miracles which
> Malachy worked. (VI, 14)
>
> ¶ Here he also healed a cleric named Michael who suf-
> fered dysentery, sending him something from his own
> table as a last resort. Later he cured the same man
> when he was grievously stricken with illness a second
> time in both body and mind. Immediately he clung to
> God and to his servant Malachy, afraid that something
> worse should happen to him if he were once again un-
> grateful for the kindliness and the miracle. (VII, 15)

¶ Malachy upon leaving us made a good journey to Scotland. He found King David, who is still in power, in one of his castles. His son lay sick to the point of death. Going into [the king] Malachy was honorably received and humbly entreated to heal his son.

He blessed water and sprinkled the youth with it and looking straight at him said: 'Have faith son; you shall not die this season.' He said this and on the following day the cure followed the word of the prophet; then the joy of the father, the shouting and uproar of the whole exulting household followed the cure. (XVII, 40)

¶ From then on they used to bring the infirm and the sick from the neighboring region and many are healed. A woman whose limbs were completely useless was brought there on a cart and she went back home on her own feet, having stayed but a single night in the holy place; not in vain did she look to the mercy of the Lord. (XVII, 41)

Many healings done by Malachy involved casting out demons. The incidents cited here, showing the ability to destroy various mental disorders, are similar to healings made by Jesus and the early Christian church.

¶ In the city of Lismore a man vexed by a demon was freed by Malachy. On another occasion as he was passing through Leinster a young child having a demon was brought to him and was taken back cured. In the same region he ordered a lunatic woman who had been found with straps to be freed and washed in water which he had blessed. She was washed and was cured.

In the region of Ulidia at Saul there was another woman whom he cured by prayer and touching her. She had been biting her own limbs with her teeth. Relatives and neighbors brought to the man of God a madman who foretold many future events. He was bound tightly with cords because his frenzies made him dangerous and terribly strong. Malachy prays over him and at once the sick man is healed and unbound. (XX, 46)

The final selection shows Malachy averting death and restoring a woman to complete health.

¶ In the neighborhood of the monastery of Bangor lived a nobleman whose wife was sick to the point of death. Malachy was begged to come down before she died, to anoint her with oil. He came down and went in to her. She rejoiced at seeing him, enlivened by the hope of health. And although he was getting ready to anoint her, everyone thought it were better to defer it until morning (it was evening.)

Malachy agreed and after blessing the sick woman he left with those who were with him. But a little while later there was suddenly a cry, weeping and great commotion throughout the house, because it was reported that she had died. Malachy came running when he heard the noise and his disciples followed him. And approaching the bed to ascertain that she had really died, Malachy was greatly perturbed in mind, blaming himself that she had passed away deprived of the grace of the Sacrament. Raising his hands to heaven, he said: 'I beseech you, O Lord, I have acted foolishly. I, it is I who have sinned; I who deferred [giving the Sacrament], it is not she, she desired it.'

This is what he said and he claimed in everyone's hearing that he would take no comfort or give any rest to his spirit, unless he were allowed to restore the grace which he had removed. He stood over her and he agonized, groaning all night, and instead of holy oil he kept pouring a great flood of tears over the dead woman, giving her that in place of holy unction. Then he spoke thus to his disciples: 'Watch and pray.' So they kept the night vigil with psalms; he with tears. Come morning the Lord heard his servant because the Spirit of the Lord was begging on his behalf, who intercedes for the saints with unspeakable groanings.

Why say more? The woman who had been dead opened her eyes, and rubbing her forehead and temples with her hands, as those do who awaken from a

deep sleep, she got up from her couch and, recognizing Malachy, she bowed devoutly and greeted him.

And as their sorrow turned into joy; they were all astonished, both those who saw it and those who heard
of it. Malachy too gave thanks, blessing the Lord. And
he anointed her nevertheless, knowing that in this
sacrament sins are forgiven and that the prayer of faith
saves the sick. After this he went off and she completely recovered. (XXIV, 53)

CHAPTER 8

FRANCIS OF ASSISI

(1182 - 1226)

The early life of Giovanni di Bernardone — later known as Francis of Assisi — gave little indication of an interest in religion. Yet before he was thirty years old, this young maverick had captured the attention of wide segments of medieval Christendom. During a relatively short lifetime he earned a reputation as "the second Christ."[1] Percy Dearmer labeled Francis as "one of the most Christlike men that ever lived."[2]

Francis was born into a prosperous merchant family. His youth was marked by wanton revelry and an extravagant display of wealth. He received little formal education, and his major hope was to become a knight in order to pursue a military career. He fought in a war between Assisi and Perugia that led to his capture and a year of imprisonment. Upon his release he became seriously ill.

This experience began a gradual transformation in Francis' motives and outlook on life. He turned increasingly to solitude and prayer. He began to feel a sense of sympathy with the poor and the sick, especially with people suffering from leprosy. This conversion became more and more focused on what Professor Jaroslav Pelikan called "the person of the historical Jesus as the Divine and Human Model."[3]

Several visions caused Francis to renounce the world and follow a life of humility and poverty. He also felt a calling to rebuild churches, an inspiration that caused him and a few followers to refurbish a small church at Portiucula, near Assisi. This church became the place where he soon founded a new monastic order. In a dramatic display in the presence of a bishop, Francis renounced his disgruntled father and returned to him all his worldly possessions.[4]

In 1209 Francis attended a church service where the priest read the following words from the book of Matthew:

> And as ye go, preach, saying, The kingdom of heaven
> is at hand. Heal the sick, cleanse the lepers, raise the
> dead, cast out devils, freely ye have received, freely
> give. Provide neither gold, nor silver, nor brass in your
> purses, nor scrip for your journey, neither two coats,
> neither shoes, nor yet staves: for the workman is wor-
> thy of his meat. (10: 7 – 10)

Jesus' appeal to renounce material wealth led Francis to follow one of
the most austere forms of self-denial in medieval Christianity. The command to heal the sick, cleanse the lepers, and cast out devils caused him to
perform numerous healings. Jesus' appeal for a life of service, charity,
and simplicity resulted in the formation of the Franciscan monastic order.

The Friars Minor ("lesser or humble brothers") started with a few loyal
followers and later became "The Franciscans." After some hesitation, the
pope approved the Friars as a recognized order. The group had a few simple rules and was held together primarily by a common vow of poverty
and the charismatic personality of its dedicated leader. Very few of Francis' disciples were ordained priests. Francis himself was only a deacon.

The order had little theology or doctrine. It discouraged secular learning since it could be used to gain worldly wealth and power. The early
Friars were anti-intellectual; no member of the order owned a book.
Their message came only in the form of preaching and a little singing.
The healings done by Francis were secondary to the vow of poverty and
service to the poor. This was the way Francis and his followers sought to
imitate the life and works of Jesus.

In 1224 Francis retired to a hermitage on a mountain near Florence
where a famous legend emerged.[5] After fasting and praying for forty
days, he had a vision which included the image of an angel, a seraph, and
the body of the crucified Jesus. When this vision disappeared, Francis'
hands, feet, and side had allegedly been pierced like the body of Jesus at
Calvary. These marks are called *stigmata*. They are believed by many
Christians to symbolize Francis' close imitation of the life of Jesus.

The Franciscan order expanded to many countries, including England,
France, Spain, Germany, and Hungary.[6] Some of its adherents opposed
the growing secularism of the medieval church and proclaimed a need
for a new "spiritual church" pursuing the purity of Jesus' teachings in the
form of absolute poverty.[7] A more moderate group of Franciscans came
under the influence of Bonaventure (1221 – 1274), who has been called
"the second founder" of the order. This Tuscan clergyman softened the
views of the order on poverty and self-mortification.

Franciscan monasteries were soon furnished with many of the same amenities as the buildings of other monastic orders. The anti-intellectualism of the early Franciscans gave way to an avid pursuit of theological and scientific studies. Some of the most penetrating denunciations of Scholasticism during the thirteenth and fourteenth centuries were made by Franciscan scholars. The English friar John Duns Scotus rejected many of Thomas Aquinas' views on the capacity of human reason to blend with Christian inspiration and revelation. Another English Franciscan, William of Ockham, went further than Duns Scotus and upheld a complete separation between human reason and Christian faith. He also separated Christian theology and the natural sciences. One historian stated: "Ockham's separation of reason from faith severed the age-long bond between theology and natural science, freeing science to follow its own independent course." [8]

Francis himself composed very few writings. Those which have survived consist mostly of rules for his monastic order, prayers, and letters. His life and ideas have been recorded in the biographies of numerous scholars during the past seven centuries. One of the first biographies was written by Thomas of Celano. It was titled *The Lives of S. Francis* and was first published in 1229. This book contains most of the reliable information about Francis' healing works.

The following excerpts are from *The Lives of S. Francis.* Like some written accounts of the healings performed by other Christian leaders such as Cuthbert, Bernard, and Malachy, these descriptions contain language and symbols used by the late medieval church to praise the lives of prominent theologians. These healings show the role of humility and a recognition that God alone is the healing power. They also reveal the importance of faith and an expectancy of healing in eradicating disease.

¶ Once when Francis the Saint of God was making a long circuit through various regions to preach the Gospel of God's kingdom he came to a city called Toscanella. Here, while he was sowing the seed of life, as he was wont, he was entertained by a knight of that same city whose only son was a cripple and weak in all his body. Though the child was of tender years, he had passed the age of weaning; but he still remained in a cradle.

But the boy's father, seeing the man of God to be endued with such holiness, humbly fell at his feet and besought him to heal his son. Francis, deeming himself to be unprofitable and unworthy of such power and grace, for a long time refused to do it. At last, conquered by the urgency of the knight's entreaties, after offering up prayer he laid his hand on the boy, blessed him, and lifted him up. And in the sight of all the boy straightway arose while in the name of our Lord Jesus Christ, and began to walk hither and thither about the house. (Chap. XXIII, para. 65)

¶ Once when Francis the man of God had come to Narni and was staying there several days, a man of that city named Peter was lying in bed paralysed. For five months he had been so completely deprived of the use of all his limbs that he could in no wise lift himself up or move at all; and thus, having lost all help from feet, hands and head, he could only move his tongue and open his eyes.

But on hearing that S. Francis was come to Narni he sent a messenger to the Bishop to ask that he would, for Divine compassion's sake, be pleased to send the servant of God Most High to him, for he trusted that he would be delivered, by the sight and presence of the Saint, from the infirmity whereby he has holden.

And so indeed it came to pass; for when the blessed Francis was come to him he made the sign of the cross over him from head to feet, and forthwith drove away all his sickness and restored him to his former health. (Chap. XXIII, para. 66)

¶ A woman of the above-named city [Gubbio] who had been struck blind was found worthy of receiving the longed-for light immediately on the blessed Francis' making the sign of the cross over her eyes.

At Gubbio there was [another] woman both whose hands were contracted so that she could do nothing with them. As soon as she knew that S. Francis had entered the city she ran to him, and with miserable and woe-begone face showed him her deformed hands and began to pray that he would deign to touch them.

He was moved with compassion, touched her hand and healed them. And straightway the woman returned joyfully to her house, made a cheesecake with her own hands and offered it to the holy man; he took a little in token of kindness, and bade her and her household eat the rest. (Chap. XXIV, para. 67)

The next passages tell of healings by Francis in overcoming the affliction of demons, a common malady in early Christianity and the Middle Ages. The healing of the demon-possessed woman at Gemini involved a strong protest against the evil causing the affliction, a practice often used by Jesus and the apostles.

¶ There was a brother who often suffered from a grievous infirmity that was horrible to see; and I know not what name to give it; though some think it was caused by a malignant devil. For oftentimes he was dashed down and with a terrible look in his eyes he wallowed foaming; sometimes his limbs were contracted, sometimes extended, sometimes they were folded and twisted together, and sometimes they became hard and rigid. Sometimes, tense and rigid all over, with his feet touching his head, he would be lifted up in the air to the height of a man's stature and would then suddenly spring back to the earth.

The holy father Francis pitying his grievous sickness went to him and after offering up prayer signed him with the cross and blessed him. And suddenly he was made whole, and never afterwards suffered from this distressing infirmity. (Chap. XXV, para. 68)

¶ One day when the most blessed father Francis was passing through the diocese of Narni he reached a fortress known as that of S. Gemini, and while he was there preaching the Gospel of God's kingdom, he with three brethren were entertained by a man who feared and worshipped God and was very well reported of in that town.

But his wife, as was known to all the inhabitants of the place, was vexed with a devil; and so her husband besought the blessed Francis for her, trusting that by his

merits she might be delivered. But S. Francis, desiring
in his simplicity rather to be had in contempt than
through ostentation of sanctity to be uplifted by the
favour of this world, altogether refused to do this
thing.

At length, since God was concerned in the case, he
yielded to the prayers of the many who were entreat-
ing him. So he called the three brethren who were with
him, and setting each one in a corner of the house, he
said to them, "Brethren, let us pray to the Lord for this
woman, that God may break off from her the devil's
yoke, to His praise and glory. Stand we apart (he
added) in the corners of the house, that this evil spirit
may not be able to escape us or delude us by trying to
sneak into the corners."

Accordingly, having finished his prayer blessed Francis went in the power of the Spirit to the woman who
was being miserably tormented and crying horribly;
and he said, "In the name of our Lord Jesus Christ, I
charge thee, devil, on obedience, to go out of her nor
dare to impede her any more."

Hardly had he finished speaking when the devil with
furious roaring rushed out so swiftly that the holy father thought himself under some illusion, because of
the sudden healing of the woman and the prompt obedience of the devil. And forthwith he departed from
that place shamefacedly, for God's providence had so
wrought in the matter that there might be no place for
vainglory on his part. (Chap. XXV, para. 69)

The final excerpt recounts another healing of demons by Francis in a
medieval Italian city. At the end, this account explains that Francis performed many healings that were not recorded. It also indicates that his
primary religious mission was promoting the rules of his monastic order
rather than doing works of physical and mental healing.

¶ At Citta di Castello also there was a woman possessed by a devil; and when the most blessed father
Francis was there she was brought to the house in
which he was staying. But she remained outside and

began to gnash her teeth, to make faces and to utter lamentable roarings, after the manner of unclean spirits; and many of the people in that city of both sexes came up and besought S. Francis for the woman; for that evil spirit had long vexed her by his torments and had troubled them by his roarings.

Then the holy father sent to her a brother who was with him, with the intention of finding out whether it really was a devil, or only a woman's deception. When the woman saw the brother she began to mock him, knowing that he was not S. Francis.

The holy father was praying within, and when he had finished his prayer he came out; and then the woman began to tremble and to roll on the ground, unable to stand his power. S. Francis called her to him and said, "In virtue of obedience I bid thee go out of her, thou unclean spirit," and he straightway left her, doing her no hurt, and departed very full of wrath.

Thanks be to God Almighty, who worketh all in all! However, since we have determined to set forth not miracles (which do not make holiness but show it), but rather the excellence of S. Francis' life and the flawless pattern of his conversation, we will omit the miracles for their abundance and return to works of eternal salvation. (Chap. XXVI, para. 70)

CHAPTER 9

CATHERINE OF SIENA

(1347 – 1380)

It is fitting that the final chapter in this chronological survey of Christian healing by individuals during the Middle Ages is about the healing works of a woman. With very few exceptions since the early healings cited in the Old Testament, the development of spiritual healing based on the Bible has been dominated by men.

Healings were certainly performed by women in the early Christian church despite the absence of their names in historical writings. In Chapter 5 of this book covering the Eastern Orthodox Church, we have cited Macrina, the sister of Basil and Gregory of Nyssa, who healed a child of defective eyesight. In this same chapter we have also mentioned "a certain woman" unnamed by the historian Socrates Scholasticus in his account of her healing work among the Iberian pagans in the region of Georgia. Other healers or biographers of healers in the written annals of Christian history have been men.

The healing works of Catherine of Siena during the fourteenth century began to change this tradition. In a relatively short period she accomplished as many impressive healings as some of the male healers in previous centuries. In many ways her achievements in Christian healing were a timely portent of the growing influence of women healers in future generations. More than she realized during her brief lifetime, Catherine set an example of an important leadership role for women in the Christian church. She also assisted in reviving the healing mission of Jesus just as increasing numbers of women have begun to do in the nineteenth and twentieth centuries.

Catherine was the most prominent "mystic" during the late Middle Ages. She led a movement toward an inner search for God combined with active service to the poor and sick. She denounced the growing secularism and corruption in the church, and called for a return to the teachings of the New Testament. Walker described this reformist trend as

> the quest for direct personal contact with God, whether through the mystical union of the soul with God or through a cultivation of the interior life — a practice of the presence of God — that did not involve actual mystical experience. Common also was the underlying conviction that the regeneration of church and society required personal religious renewal: a religion of true inwardness rather than of mere conformity to outward rites and ceremonies. [1]

Catherine Benincasa was the twenty-third child in a family of little wealth or rank. Few of her brothers and sisters lived to adulthood; her twin sister died only a few days after their birth. Her father was a dyer of cloth and a member of the "popolo minuto," the lower classes of Italian society who were slowly gaining some prosperity and social standing. It was a time of severe instability and hardship. The black plague was beginning to spread beyond the port cities of Italy, and civil conflict was rampant between the Vatican and a number of papal states. A bitter schism within the church had kept the Roman pope in a palace at Avignon in France for more than seventy years.

From her early youth, Catherine was intensely religious. In spite of the troubled times, she had a deep sense of joy and inexhaustible energy. Her family wanted her to get married as soon as she reached her early teens, but she insisted on following a life of service to the church. To discourage suitors, she shaved off her hair and spent more time in solitude and prayer. At first she was ridiculed by her family, which caused her to develop a sense of inner strength and conviction. One writer explained that Catherine found the need early in life to build "an interior cell into which one can retire to be alone with God." [2] This cell, she declared, was "simply self-knowledge in God."

Catherine's father relented and provided her with a room in their home where she spent three years in quiet contemplation. [3] She often fasted, and she taught herself to read the Bible and other religious writings. A strong fascination with the early desert fathers came from this study, and she desired to imitate their solitary life. At eighteen Catherine joined a special group for women in the Dominican order, where she met Raymond of Capua, the General of this clerical organization. Raymond became her spiritual tutor and he was later one of her first biographers.

As a member of the Dominicans, Catherine became active in ministering to the sick and poor. She aided in converting non-believers to the church, including important persons in Siena, Pisa, and Florence. In 1374 she helped many people suffering from the black plague. It was at this difficult time that she healed a number of persons through her faith and prayer. One of those healed was her mentor, Raymond of Capua.

As a reformer Catherine spoke out against the church for its pursuit of wealth and power as well as its oppression of the poor. She kept an active correspondence with numerous kings, queens, princes, and a variety of other notable officials throughout Europe in an attempt to quell civil violence and injustice. In an effort to end the schism in the church, she went to Avignon and persuaded Pope Gregory XI to return to Rome despite the opposition of many cardinals. The pope later sent her on a mission appealing for peace among several papal enemies. By more letters and personal appeals, Catherine gained support for a new pope (Urban VI) from church leaders in Germany, Hungary, and Sweden. [4]

Catherine composed very few religious writings. Just before her death she dictated her "Dialogue" which contained many of her ideas on Christian theology. A portion of this work was titled *The Book of Divine Doctrine*. More than forty biographies about Catherine's life had been written when the English author, Josephine Butler, wrote her well-known biography in 1868. The early biographies were written by Raymond of Capua and other authors during Catherine's lifetime. Some of these biographies are good sources for information on her healing works. One of the best accounts of the healings by Catherine is included in the biography by Mrs. Butler.

The following excerpts are from *Catherine of Siena,* by Josephine Butler. Some of the descriptions of healing are narrations made by observers who accompanied Catherine on her religious mission.

The first account relates a healing of Catherine's mother, who was given up by the physicians and expected to die. This incident occurred just after the death of Catherine's father.

> ¶ In 1372 good Giacomo, Catherine's father, died. While the family all wept around his bed, Catherine alone remained calm and even joyful, for she realized the fulness of peace into which her beloved father had entered.
>
> Then Lapa [Catherine's mother] fell ill, and drew near to death. She was a true and simple-hearted Christian, but she dearly loved life, and revolted against the

thought of dying. She besought her daughter to obtain for her the favour of a longer life.

Catherine, seeing her mother so far from resigned to the will of God, and too much devoted to the things of the earth, retired to her room, and prayed earnestly that her beloved mother might live and become more prepared for the kingdom of God. The physicians had already pronounced Lapa's malady to be past cure; but she recovered, and lived till her ninetieth year. (p. 94)

The next incident describes the healing of a clergyman in Siena during the black plague.

¶ The good Raymond of Capua must be first mentioned; he tells us himself of his introduction to Catherine. "In 1373 I was summoned to Siena, where I exercised the function of lector in the convent of my order, that of the Dominicans. I was serving God in a cold and formal manner, when the plague broke out in Siena, where it raged with greater violence that in any other city. Terror reigned everywhere. Zeal for souls, which is the essence of the spirit of St. Dominic, urged me to labour for the salvation of my neighbours.

"I necessarily went very often to the Hospital of la Misericordia. The director of that hospital at that time was Father Matthew of Cenni, an attached friend of Catherine. Every morning, on my way to the city, I inquired at the Misericordia whether any more of the inmates there had been attacked with the plague.

"One day on entering, I saw some of the brothers carrying Father Matthew like a corpse from the chapel to his room; his face was livid, and his strength was so far gone that he could not answer me when I spoke to him. 'Last night,' the brothers said, 'about eleven o'clock, while ministering to a dying person, he perceived himself stricken, and fell at once into extreme weakness.'

"I helped to lay him on his bed; . . . he spoke afterwards, and said that he felt as if his head was separating into four parts. I sent for Dr. Senso, his physician;

Dr. Senso declared to me that my friend had the plague, and that every symptom announced the approach of death. 'I fear,' he said, 'that the House of Mercy (Misericordia) is about to be deprived of its good director.' I asked if medical art could not save him; 'We shall see,' replied Dr. Senso, 'but I have only a very faint hope; his blood is too much poisoned.'

"I withdrew, praying God to save the life of this good man. Catherine, however, had heard of the illness of Father Matthew, whom she loved sincerely, and she lost no time in repairing to him. The moment she entered the room, she cried, with a cheerful voice, 'Get up, Father Matthew, get up! This is not a time to be lying idly in bed.'

"Father Matthew roused himself, sat up on his bed, and finally stood on his feet. Catherine retired; at the moment she was leaving the house, I entered it, and ignorant of what had happened, and believing my friend to be still at the point of death, my grief urged me to say, 'Will you allow a person so dear to us, and so useful to others to die?'

"She appeared annoyed at my words, and replied: 'In what terms do you address me? Am I like God, to deliver a man from death?' But I, beside myself with sorrow, pleaded, 'Speak in that way to others if you will, but not to me; for I know your secrets: and *I know that you obtain from God whatsoever you ask in faith.*' Then Catherine bowed her head, and smiled just a little; after a few moments she lifted up her head and looked full in my face, her countenance radiant with joy, and said: 'Well, let us take courage; he will not die this time;' and she passed on.

"At these words I banished all fear, for I understood that she had obtained some favour from heaven. I went straight to my sick friend, whom I found sitting on the side of his bed. 'Do you know', he cried, 'what she has done for me?' He then stood up and joyfully narrated what I have here written.

"To make the matter more sure, the table was laid, and
Father Matthew seated himself at it with us; they
served him with vegetables and other light food, and
he who an hour before could not open his mouth, ate
with us, chatting and laughing gaily. Great was our joy
and admiration; we all thanked and praised God. Nicolas d'Andrea, of the Friar Preachers, was there, besides students, priests, and more than twenty other persons, who all saw and heard what I have narrated."
(pp. 97 – 98)

The next excerpt consists of a general commentary on Catherine's attitude toward Christian healing. Her methods included prayer, a deep
faith in God's power to heal, and the use of confessing one's sins. This
discussion also contains some interesting observations on the spiritual
healing during the period of early Christianity and its later decline caused
by a "decay of the faith." The renewal of faith and prayer, it explains,
should be able to revive the practice of Christian healing in the future.

¶ Catherine's prayers brought health to many sick persons. She believed in the promise, "The prayer of faith
shall save the sick;" and doubted not its fulfilment in
answer to earnest prayer, in every case in which that
fulfilment was for the good of the sufferer and for the
glory of God. The other methods she employed, besides the all-powerful one of prayer, were to persuade
the patient to make a full confession of sin, then to
speak peace to his conscience, through faith in Jesus
Christ, and to inspire him with a joyous courage and
resolution.

Physicians well know how closely connected is bodily
health with mental conditions; but most will question
the power even of the highest faith to arrest the progress
of a poison actually working in the blood. Into such
questions it is not my present intention to enter; my part
is to present a simple narrative, concerning which those
who read may draw their own conclusions.

After our Lord Jesus Christ had ascended to heaven,
the first apostles received, together with many other
spiritual gifts, showered down on the day of Pentecost,

such gifts of healing, that the sick were brought by
their friends and laid in the streets of Jerusalem, that
perchance the shadow only of Peter passing by might
overshadow them and restore them to health and life.

No historian of the Church has yet ventured to assign
an exact date to the cessation of the so-called miraculous gifts of healing; perhaps when we see all things
more clearly, we shall know that these gifts only
ceased in proportion to the decay of the faith which
claimed and exercised them; and we may be able
again by prayer of faith to heal the sick and cast out
evil spirits. (pp. 98 – 99)

The next brief passage tells how Catherine restored the narrator of
some of these healings. He was her good friend, Raymond of Capua.

¶ Father Raymond then recounts how, having fallen ill
himself through his excessive exertions in the plague-
stricken city, he crawled to Catherine's house, where
not being able longer to stand up, he fell prostrate, and
lay half-conscious till she returned from her labours;
how she, placing both her pure hands on his forehead,
remained absorbed in prayer for an hour and a half,
how he fell into a peaceful slumber, and how on awak-
ing in perfect health, she said to him, "Go now, and
labour for the salvation of souls, and render thanks to
the Lord who has saved you from this great danger."
(p. 99)

After her visit to Avignon, where she helped resolve a serious split
within the church, Catherine left the pope's palace and traveled to
Toulon. The next account describes a healing she performed while making this journey. It gives a good indication of her widespread reputation
as an effective healer.

¶ Catherine had parted from [Pope] Gregory at Avignon, to pursue a route of her own, with her companions, to Toulon. Her journey was much more expedi-
tious than that of the Pontiff: it was unimpeded by
regrets, murmurings, or hesitations. She set out with a
cheerful heart, and full of hope. . . .

She remained for two days at Toulon. She and her
companions arrived there towards evening, when she
immediately retired to her room to pray, as was her
unvarying custom at the evening hour . . . They had
not been there for an hour, when a numerous multitude of women gathered round the door of the inn,
asking where the saint was who had come from the
pontifical court. . . . The foremost among the women
pressed into the vestibule of the inn; but Catherine remained concealed in her chamber.

One of the women, who was very retiring and care-
worn in appearance, carried in her arms her sick baby,
a pitiful object, but *her* treasure. She besought the
friends of Catherine that she would take the infant in
her arms and cure it; 'for,' she said, 'she has power
with God, and can heal diseases: she can restore to me
my baby which is dying.'

The message was taken to Catherine, but she declined
to undertake this, or to appear; for she dreaded the
publicity of the occasion. But the entreaties and sobs
of the poor mother, whose petitions were seconded by
the other women, were too much for her compassionate heart: she came out of her chamber, and said,
'Where is the little one?'

The mother pressed forward, and Catherine, full of
pity, took the baby in her arms, and, pressing it to her
breast, she prayed earnestly and with tears to him who
said, 'Suffer the little children to come unto me.' From
that moment the child revived, and the whole city was
witness of its rapid return to health, and of the joy of
the poor mother. (pp. 190 – 191)

The final passages tell of healings done by Catherine during a visit to
the city of Genoa. They show again the advantage of spiritual healing
over the limited knowledge and capabilities of the medical profession of
the time.

¶ Catherine and her friends remained more than a
month at Genoa, at the house of an honourable lady

named Orietta Scott. Stephen [a friend of Catherine's] says, in his deposition: 'We were nearly all sick while there. Neri di Landoccio fell ill first. He suffered dreadful pain; he could neither lie in bed nor stand up, but would crawl about on his hands and knees all night while other people rested, and thus increased his pains. When Catherine heard of it she was filled with compassion, and ordered Father Raymond to call in the best medical aid. He promptly brought two skillful physicians, who prescribed for Neri; but he became no better.'

Raymond says, 'We were all at dinner when the news came to us that Neri was rather worse than better. Stephen ceased to eat; he looked very sad, and, leaving the table, went straight to Catherine's room. He threw himself at her feet, and with tears adjured her not to suffer his dear friend, who had undertaken this journey for God and for her, to die far from his family, and be buried in a strange city.'

Catherine was deeply affected; she said: 'If God wills, Stephen, that your friend should thus reap the reward of his labours, you ought not to be afflicted, but rather to rejoice.' But Stephen insisted: 'O dearest, kindest mother, hear my request. You *can* do it if you will; you can obtain this favour from God.'

Catherine replied, with a look full of pity, 'I only exhorted you to conform to God's will. To-morrow, when I go to receive the Communion, remind me of your request, and I will pray to the Lord for Neri; and meanwhile do you pray without ceasing for his recovery.' Stephen did not fail to throw himself in her path as she went to the church, and said: 'Mother, I entreat you not to deceive my expectations.'

Catherine remained an unusually long time in the church, in prayer. When she returned, she smiled on Stephen, who was waiting for her, and said, 'Be of good cheer, my son; you have obtained the favour you have sought.' Stephen, not quite able to believe for joy, eagerly asked, 'Will Neri get well?' 'Undoubtedly he will,' Catherine replied.

In a few days Neri was quite well. But Stephen, worn out by his fatigues in nursing the patients, and by his anxiety about his beloved friend, was attacked by a violent fever. 'As every one loved him, says Raymond, 'we resorted to him to try and console him, and all nursed him by turns.'

Stephen himself gave the following account of it: 'Catherine came, with her companions, to pay me a visit, and asked me what I was suffering. I, quite delighted at her sweet presence, answered gaily, 'They *say* I am ill; but I do not know what it is.' She placed her hand on my forehead; and shaking her head and smiling, she said, 'do you hear how this child answers me? — They *say* that I am ill, but I do not know of what; — and he is in a violent fever!' then she added, addressing me: 'But, Stephen, I do not allow you to be ill; you must get up and wait upon the others as before.'

She then conversed with us about God, as usual, and as she was speaking I began to feel quite well. I interrupted her to tell them so, and they were all in astonishment, and very glad. I arose from my bed the same day, and I have enjoyed perfect health since that time. (pp. 204 – 205)

For God sent not his Son into the world

to condemn the world;

but that the world through him might be saved.

John

PART THREE

THE EMERGENCE OF FAVORABLE CONDITIONS

IN THE LATE MIDDLE AGES

FOR A RESTORATION OF CHRISTIAN HEALING

PART THREE

By the end of the Middle Ages several important trends had emerged in Christian healing. Spiritual healing based on the Bible continued after the fourth century, yet it was achieved by individual Christians rather than as an accepted practice of the medieval church. The historical period covered in this survey shows that some of the most important leaders of the medieval church who shaped its theology and doctrines for many centuries were also major recorders of healings performed by lesser known Christians. A few leading theologians such as Augustine and Bernard did healing works themselves in addition to writing about the healings done by others.

Our survey also reveals that most of these healings were accomplished during the early part of the Middle Ages, a period labeled by many historians as "the Dark Ages." Spiritual healing declined markedly after the year 1000 when the medieval church became more powerful, more secular, and less spiritually oriented.

Christian healing was not an integral part of the medieval church as it was in the early church. It was achieved intermittently during the Middle Ages by a very small number of spiritually-minded clergy. Yet they did not endeavor to restore an understanding of spiritual healing in their preaching or writings. Nor did they teach other Christians how to heal or maintain a healing mission. For these reasons there were long gaps of time between individual Christians doing healing works after the eighth century.

Throughout the entire medieval era all Christians who practiced spiritual healing acknowledged that their ability came from God and the teachings of Jesus; they never claimed any personal power of their own. At times some healers such as Bernard, Francis, and Catherine were reluctant to heal, declaring they had no capability of their own to destroy disease. Only after much pleading by people in urgent need did they perform another healing.

A few key questions emerge from this chronological survey of Christian healing. What conditions enabled a few individual Christians to continue with spiritual healing after the time of the early church? How were these men and women different from other Christians? How were they able to follow Jesus' words: "Heal the sick, cleanse the lepers, raise the dead, cast out devils?" As the title of this book suggests, what lessons in Christian healing are relevant for the historical period *beyond* the Middle Ages?

A chief factor in the continuation of spiritual healing after the time of the early Christian church was the development of monasticism. As the medieval church filled the power vacuum left by the Roman Empire and became increasingly secular, some Christians sought refuge from this worldly trend by isolating themselves in secluded locations. They wanted to preserve the spiritual fervor and dedication that had motivated Jesus and the apostles.

This small clerical movement had access to the Bible. Their members included the few literate people of their time. They devoted long hours to meditation and prayer. Their monasteries became important centers of study and learning. Almost all individuals involved in Christian healing were far removed from the environs of Rome and the intense power struggles and expanding wealth surrounding the papacy.

At the same time the medieval healers maintained contact with society. They did not totally cut themselves off from people seeking physical healing or spiritual instruction. In the Egyptian desert, many people came from far and near to the remote retreats of healers such as Anthony and Hilarion. Later in Western Europe, healers like Cuthbert, Bernard, and Catherine went out from their places of meditation and prayer and healed people in nearby communities.

These forms of Christian monasticism were successors of an important practice of the early Christian church. Jesus, the apostles, and the first church fathers often went into the desert or mountains to be alone with God and to seek His inspiration and guidance. Thereafter they went out among the villages and cities to preach and to heal.

Christian monasticism was also a form of protest against the spreading secularization of the medieval church. In varying degrees, the men and women who continued to heal the sick were not influenced solely by the dogma, superstition, and ritualism which enveloped Western society for almost 1200 years. Some of these persons were ridiculed for their works of healing. In spite of its enormous influence in weakening the mission of Christian healing, the papacy paradoxically made some acknowledgement of the healing works of these gifted Christian leaders and canonized them as saints. In the preface to her book titled *Christian Healing*, Evelyn Frost commented on this historical development as follows:

> The most fruitful fields for research in the matter of
> Christian healing are the first three centuries of the

Christian era, whilst all through the subsequent history
of the church miracles of healing are to be found. . .
Throughout history there have almost always been
found individuals who have used this key [the spiritual
message of the early church] and with it have opened
the door of physical healing for others, but they have
often been regarded as exceptional or even eccentric
people, 'saints' as contrasted with the 'rank and file'
of Christians. [1]

Three Conditions for the Restoration
of Healing in the Christian Church

Another important question also arises from this historical survey:
Where will spiritual healing in the Christian church be restored? What
conditions will be needed to revive the healing mission started by Jesus
and the early Christian church? The healing works by individual Christians during the Middle Ages would certainly be continued by spiritually-minded Christians after the end of the medieval era. In time, new efforts would certainly be made to reestablish spiritual healing within the
teachings and practices of the Christian church.

Yet to restore Christian healing on a stable and permanent basis, a favorable social environment would be needed. The works of gifted healers from the very start of Christianity served as seeds attempting to germinate and grow as sturdy plants for the nourishment and advancement
of mankind. What was lacking from the time of Jesus was a suitable soil
for these seeds of love and healing and proof to send down deep and im-
perishable roots.

By 1500 the restoration of Christian healing in the territories of its origin was very unlikely. The places where Jesus and the apostles began
their healing mission were now largely inhabited by Arab Moslems. The
same condition existed in former Christian centers in North Africa where
Anthony, Hilarion, Augustine, and other healers had lived. Cities and
towns in Asia Minor and Greece where the Apostle Paul had performed
many wonderful healings had just been conquered by Turkish Moslems.
The mental atmosphere in the papal states and other territories surrounding Rome was especially adverse to a renewal of Jesus' mission of spiritual healing.

Under these conditions the restoration of spiritual healing would likely
emerge in an area of Christendom where a deeper understanding of the

Bible could be fostered along with the evolution of a higher concept of the dignity and freedom of man. It would be a place where the rigid clericalism of the medieval church was reducing its hold on the minds of increasing numbers of people. It would be a region where thinking Christians were eager to move into a new phase in the development of their revolutionary religion.

The permanent establishment of Christian healing, I suggest, would come in a social environment where three conditions prevail: 1) public access to the Bible, 2) the institutionalization of individual freedom, and 3) a culture embracing religious tolerance.

By the end of the Middle Ages the first two of these conditions were beginning to emerge in modest degree in northern Europe or in England. The third condition for religious tolerance was essentially weak and undeveloped everywhere in Western Europe.

I. *Public Access to the Bible*

During the latter part of the fifteenth century the medieval church lost its ability to confine access to the Bible to the clergy. Increasing numbers of people were becoming familiar with the spiritual and moral messages contained in the Old and New Testaments. A new religious attitude slowly evolved that in time would be more favorable to a revival of Christian healing.

This major development in Western civilization was assisted by the translation of the Bible into national languages and by the invention of the printing press. Christian learning and salvation soon became an individual matter; each man, woman, and child by himself or herself could turn to the Scriptures for an understanding of his or her relationship to God. No longer was this important learning process a monopoly of the church or the clergy.

Some portions of the Bible and other religious literature had been translated into the vernacular at earlier periods of the Middle Ages. German translations of parts of the *Vulgate* were made in the ninth century when Charlemagne sought to educate the clergy and spread some knowledge of Christianity among his people. Parts of the Bible were also translated into local languages in the Netherlands, France, and in some of the German states during the fourteenth century. Yet the first high quality translation of the entire Bible in northern Europe was the German version begun by Martin Luther in 1522. This achievement marked a big step in the Protestant Reformation.

In no country in Western Europe was the translation of the Bible into the vernacular more effective in loosening the grip of the medieval church and in gaining new freedoms than in England. In this unique island society the struggle to translate the Bible into English was closely tied to the formation of a new national culture and a new national language. This conflict was a core issue in the efforts of the English kings and people to free themselves from the ecclesiastical control of the papacy. This contest fostered a deep attachment among the English people to the teachings of the Old and New Testaments, and it led to numerous English translations of the Scriptures. [2]

The Venerable Bede had translated some parts of the New Testament into Old English in 735. King Alfred himself translated some parts of the Bible during his reign from 871 to 899.

The first effort to translate the entire Bible into the English language was made by John Wycliffe (1330 – 1384). Wycliffe's Bible consisted largely of a translation of the *Vulgate*. It was produced by several scholars, although Wycliffe himself inspired and directed the entire project. In many ways Wycliffe's purpose in translating and publishing an English version of the complete Bible transcended the scholarly achievement of putting the Scriptures into his native language. His dominant goal was a major transformation of religion and society in England. One Bible historian wrote:

> Wycliffe set himself to rethink the whole question of
> the basis of society, with special reference to the status
> of the Church. The organization of the Church as a
> feudal hierarchy seemed to him to be a great mistake,
> as also did the rich endowments which it enjoyed, a
> condition of affairs for which he could find no New
> Testament precedent. . . . The Bible was to him the
> rule of faith and practice, including ecclesiastical practice,
> for he did not conceive that the Bible's guidance
> on questions of church order and organization could
> be ambiguous. But if every man was responsible to
> obey the Bible, as the codification of the law of God, it
> followed that every man must know what to obey.
> Therefore the whole Bible should be accessible to him
> in a form that he could understand. [3]

Wycliffe's translation of the Bible was followed in fairly rapid succession by other English translations. With the assistance of Luther's Bible,

William Tyndale (1494 – 1536) made an excellent English version of the New Testament, an act which led to his execution by the church. In 1535 Myles Coverdale (1488 – 1569) published an English translation of the Bible that was used by Henry VIII in his opposition to the religious authority of the Roman church.

Other Bible translations were made by English scholars culminating in 1611 with the King James version, which has exerted an enormous impact on the expansion of religious and political thought far beyond the geographical territory of England. Since its first publication this translation has become the most widely read book in the history of the world. Professor Laura Wild declared: "No one influence has been so great in the life of English-speaking people, religiously, morally, socially, politically, as has this version." [4]

The invention of the printing press by Johann Gutenberg in Germany in 1456 was another monumental development in providing direct access to the Bible for an increasing number of people. The first book printed by this new revolutionary method was a translation of the *Vulgate*, which was called "the Gutenberg Bible." In 1475 William Caxton established a printing press in England where he began publishing different religious and philosophical writings, including the Bible, at relatively low prices. [5]

The innovation of the printing press and the translation of the Bible into national languages were prime factors ending the Middle Ages and beginning the Protestant Reformation. Walls of ignorance and superstition began tumbling down as growing numbers of Christian laymen obtained a better knowledge of the world and of themselves. Technical and commercial knowledge also expanded. A standard of living formerly enjoyed by only a small wealthy elite became available to more people.

Public access to the Bible and growing literacy enabled more Christians to become familiar with the history, victories, tribulations, poetry, proverbs, allegories, and parables contained in the Old and New Testaments. Previously they had known the stories in the Bible largely by observing their portrayal in stained glass windows in their churches and cathedrals. Now they could understand more of the meaning of these Biblical narratives through their own reading and study.

The Bible informed its readers of the dignity of man made in God's likeness. It explained God's covenant with His people and the nature of His spiritual and moral law. This law had enormous social and political significance. It upheld individual equality, human rights, and the idea of progress. It also included the vital concept of individual freedom.

II. *The Institutionalization of Individual Freedom*

A second condition required for the revival of Christian healing is a system of government and law capable of protecting the rights of individual freedom. The explanation of this condition may seem at times to digress from our chief subject matter of spiritual healing, yet it is important in understanding the gradual evolution of a social and religious atmosphere favorable to Christian healing.

The institutionalization of individual freedom involves the preservation and advancement of basic human rights by the impersonal rule of government institutions rather than the arbitrary rule of personal government leaders. It is a crucial part of a political system embodying an effective yet limited executive, an elected and representative legislature, and an independent judiciary. Under this kind of system people are governed by the rule of law rather than the rule of men.

The institutionalization of individual freedom is a basic requirement for the permanent establishment of Christian healing because spiritual healing based on the Bible needs protection from opposing groups and influences in society. The healing of disease by the use of prayer and an understanding of God is readily welcomed by persons who are in need of healing and by many others who see it as a promising proof of Christian teachings. Yet Christian healing has frequently been resisted by various opponents in society who see it as a threat to their own religious or secular views — Christian or non-Christian — and who are sometimes envious of their own inability to rely on spiritual means for similar kinds of healing.

The history of Christianity shows many examples of bitter opposition to spiritual healing and the need to protect this form of religious practice by an impersonal system of law. Jesus met this kind of hostility on many occasions. He was once chastized by the ruler of a synagogue for healing a woman on the sabbath who had suffered from a severe form of arthritis for eighteen years. (Luke 13: 11 – 17) Just after he healed a man with a withered hand, the book of Matthew relates: "Then the Pharisees went out, and held a council against him, how they might destroy him." (12: 14) On one occasion the Apostle Paul healed a man who had been crippled from birth. Soon thereafter some Jews and local people stoned him senseless and apparently near death. The prayers of his own followers revived him and the intrepid missionary continued in his work of preaching and healing. (Acts 14: 8 – 20)

Similar opposition confronted the preaching and healing of other apostles and church leaders during the time of early Christianity and throughout the Middle Ages. Christian healing has been especially galling to its critics when claims are made that healing disease by spiritual means constitutes a form of proof of the validity of Jesus' teachings. And at times there has been justifiable criticism of persons, both Christian and non-Christian, who have attempted to perform healing works with little genuine spiritual understanding only for fame and money.

The restoration and expansion of spiritual healing can consequently be achieved only in a social and legal environment embodying the institutionalized protection of individual freedom. This element of a free society provides organized and lawful channels for making public policy, including the right to protest against the status quo and existing social injustices. Only by this free and legitimate method of representative government can progress toward higher levels of freedom be achieved for each individual and for an entire society. A sufficient level of political liberty and civil justice is required for the evolution of religious freedom and the practice of Christian healing.

The institutionalization of individual freedom by 1500 was not highly developed anywhere in Europe. Yet some elements of the foundation of an impersonal system of government and law were taking form in one country where religious, political, and individual freedom would develop soon after the beginning of the Protestant Reformation.

This country was England.

A movement toward a more favorable environment for Christian healing came from three institutions emerging in English society.

The first governmental office to develop toward institutionalized authority was the monarchy. From the reign of King Alfred in the ninth century until the demise of King George III in the early nineteenth century, the monarchy tended to exercise much power. The English people supported the royal ruler as the dominant influence in the administration of the affairs of the kingdom. A good king or queen usually resulted in good government.

Yet throughout the history of England, new challenges and new needs imposed increasing limitations on the power of the monarchy. These moves gradually expanded the protection of individual freedom. During the reign of Henry I (1100 – 1135) a coronation charter known as "the Charter of Liberties" was issued by the king to gain the support of leading noblemen. [6] This measure reduced the arbitrary practices of a former monarch.

An important check on royal authority was the Magna Carta or Great

Charter signed by King John at Runnymede in 1215. This document was not a major democratic statement nor a declaration of broad noble ideals upholding individual liberty. Instead the Magna Carta was largely a reaffirmation of the property rights under feudal law of a group of disgruntled barons who were opposed to personal abuses of royal power by the king. The signing of this agreement was a modest step toward a limited exercise of executive power. Winston Churchill wrote that the Magna Carta added "a system of checks and balances which would accord the monarchy its necessary strength, but would prevent its perversion by a tyrant or a fool."[7] Significant limitations on the monarchy were also made during the reign of influential medieval kings such as Henry III, Edward I, Edward II, Edward III, and Henry VII.

The English monarchy remained strong during the Middle Ages. Yet the king was expected to uphold the custom that he should be under God and the law. He was thereby expected to share power with other institutions of government serving the welfare of the English people. By the reign of Henry VII (1485 – 1509) the English monarchy was becoming an integral part of a more institutionalized and divided form of government. One historian stated:

> The tortoise of institutional change pays slight heed to the random, if brilliant, antics of the dynastic hare. Under Henry VII a new attitude of mind was at work, a new approach to government that had little to do with victory on the battlefield or the death of kings. In the medieval past, government had been viewed primarily as a necessary evil; by the sixteenth century, men were beginning to whisper the extraordinary proposition that it might be a positive good. . . . The ameobalike quality of the feudal past, in which there was little or no distinction among the legislative, executive, and judicial aspects of government, was slowly giving way to a more precise notion of governmental function.[8]

Parliament was the second governmental institution emerging in England during the Middle Ages that was to play a growing role in protecting individual freedom. This body developed in the thirteenth century from consultations between the king and selected representatives of the upper classes regarding the taxes of the kingdom. The French word *parler* meaning "to speak" was applied to these meetings where the king usually asked his wealthy subjects for more money. In time the parliament became a major check on royal power as well as an institution providing increasing representation to broader segments of English society.

The chief method used by parliament to limit the monarchy was to increase its role in the collection and expenditure of public funds. This process became more institutionalized as this body evolved into a bicameral legislature. The House of Lords represented the church and the landed aristocracy. It often served as an advisory body to the king and as a court of final appeal. The House of Commons represented the "middle class" of this period. It made petitions to the king in the name of "the people" and it gained more influence in the administration of public finances. Legislation for government funds soon originated in the lower house, and all members of parliament were granted immunity from arrest. The national legislature gained the right to veto the king's appointments of important officials in the royal household. No longer could the king declare war without parliamentary approval.

The institutionalization of executive and legislative authority in England was the first development toward constitutional government and the protection of individual freedom in Western civilization. Nothing like this was done elsewhere in Europe before 1500. Absolutism was firmly entrenched almost everywhere on the continent, and no effective limits were placed on royal power.

France had no national legislature representing its people or protecting their individual freedom. The French parliament gave some voice to the clergy, nobility, and bourgeoisie during the late Middle Ages, and these groups held intermittent consultations with the king. Yet this body never gained genuine legislative power. During the reign of strong monarchs it was powerless. It held no sessions from the early seventeenth century until the outbreak of the French Revolution in 1789. The National Assembly formed after the Napoleonic era did not exercise significant governing power until the formation of the Third Republic in 1870.

Even less progress in institutionalizing political power was made in the German states of central Europe. A national legislature called the Reichstag was set up by Bismarck in the 1870's, yet it remained a rubber-stamp governing body. Executive and legislative institutions floundered in Germany during the Weimar Republic from 1919 to 1933. The weakness of democracy and individual freedom aided the rise of Nazi tyranny and Adolph Hitler. The German people did not really gain the ability to govern themselves by the rule of law and protect their individual freedom until the formation of the Federal Republic in West Germany after

World War II.

Only in smaller countries on the continent such as Switzerland and the Netherlands was some progress made in establishing constitutional government and the protection of individual freedom, although most of these developments did not occur until the eighteenth and nineteenth centuries.

It is important to emphasize that England started its development toward institutionalized constitutional government in the twelfth century. This island society preceded other Western countries by at least five or six hundred years in forming a social and legal environment conducive to the restoration of Christian healing.

The third institution of government that had enormous influence on the development of individual freedom in England was its unique court system and the tradition of common law. This institution emerged only in England and later spread to the governmental systems in many English colonies including Canada, Australia, New Zealand, and the United States. From their beginning during the reign of Henry II (1154 – 1189), the English courts and their standards of justice were oriented toward the rights and freedom of the individual. The legal systems on the European continent, in contrast, were founded largely on Roman civil law with its heavy emphasis on the rights and authority of the state.

Common law is based on the customs of the people. Its decisions in specific cases are derived from precedents made in similar court proceedings in the past. At first it was administered through Courts of Common Plea held by itinerant judges who traveled throughout the kingdom and gradually extended a common judicial system to all areas of local government. The itinerant judges were eventually replaced by justices of the peace appointed by the king.

Common law courts became more specialized as a Court of King's Bench was set up to handle criminal cases, and a Court of the Exchequer was established to adjudicate cases involving royal finances. Near the end of the Middle Ages some areas of common law were superseded by statutory laws that were passed by the king and parliament. The English legal system also developed a special kind of law called "equity law," which dealt with extenuating circumstances in cases where a purely procedural application of common law might result in a miscarriage of justice.

By the end of the medieval era the English court system was only partially developed according to modern standards. The courts were not equally available to all people, and access to judicial proceedings was largely dependent on a person's status and wealth. English justice for the most part was open only to the upper and middle classes.

Yet the English courts and the system of common law were becoming another bulwark against the arbitrary use of royal power. Common law was instrumental in developing the challenging responsibility whereby the monarch was "the fountain of justice" and "the protector of the law," and at the same time the ruling king or queen was under the law.

The courts and common law, in effect, supplemented the expanding power of parliament in protecting the rights and freedom of the people. Common law upheld the right to a trial by jury and the right to a speedy trial. It bolstered the movement toward a strong and independent judiciary.

This system of justice was gradually becoming one of England's most important achievements prior to 1500. It would later be one of its major contributions to Western civilization. In spite of numerous imperfections, the English courts and common law were giving increasing meaning to the concept of the dignity of the individual. In time the expanding rights of "free Englishmen" would assist in forming a social environment favorable to the revival of Christian healing.

III. *A Culture Embracing Religious Tolerance*

Religious tolerance may be defined as a sympathetic and respectful attitude toward different religious beliefs. This condition depends on a sense of genuine liberality and goodwill in interacting with people who adhere to diverse religious doctrines. It affirms the great advantages of a society where there is a diversity of religious thought and behavior. At the same time, religious tolerance implies some kind of limits on certain religious practices that may restrict the opportunity of *all* people to believe and practice their religion without fear or intimidation.

Religious tolerance overlaps with the institutionalization of individual freedom as discussed previously. In the civil and political realm, religious tolerance is closely related to religious freedom that can be protected by law. Yet religious tolerance assumes a much broader social influence than the official affairs of law and government. It requires the same respect for diverse religious convictions in private relationships such as in the family, schools, economic associations, and social organizations. Religious tolerance cannot be enforced everywhere by governmental authorities, and it depends on an open-mindedness in the shared behavior of a society. The fundamental source of religious tolerance is in the hearts and minds of the people. Bigotry and intolerance in private areas of our lives may restrict freedom of religious thought and practice as severely as oppressive laws by the government.

A certain amount of religious tolerance is also needed within a single church or religious order. In spite of a common loyalty to specific religious teachings, there is always a requirement for some variation in individual interpretations of the Bible and basic denominational principles. In a sense, religious tolerance is a special kind of expression of Christian love.

Religious tolerance of a fairly high level is required for establishing and advancing the mission of Christian healing. It prescribes a genuine acknowledgement and respect for a specific application of Jesus' teachings.

As already mentioned, this condition was weak throughout most of Christendom near the end of the Middle Ages. In many areas of Europe it was non-existent. For centuries the medieval church had imposed a rigid conformity through its extensive network of churches, monasteries, and clergy. Theological deviations were generally punished by excommunication.

More drastic measures were used by the church to enforce doctrinal conformity and to eradicate heresy after the twelfth century. This effort became increasingly severe as anticlericalism expanded because of corruption in the church, growing popular demands for social and economic change, and the rise of strong national leaders.

The Roman church responded to this challenge with the Inquisition. It employed brutal repression in an attempt to preserve its power and authority. In the name of Christianity, the medieval church during the next three centuries imprisoned, tortured, and executed many more Christians than the Roman emperors had done in their abortive efforts to stamp out the early church. The widespread fear generated by this draconian policy had a strong impact in discouraging significant developments toward religious tolerance. Durant is especially severe in his criticism of the medieval Inquisition. He wrote:

> Compared with the persecution of heresy in Europe from 1227 to 1492, the persecution of Christians by Romans in the first three centuries after Christ was a mild and humane procedure. Making every allowance required of an historian and permitted to a Christian, we must rank the Inquisition, along with the wars and persecutions of our time, as among the darkest blots on the record of mankind, revealing a ferocity unknown in any beast. [9]

It is no accident that the Protestant Reformation first emerged in territories where the Inquisition was relatively weak. These areas were England, the Netherlands, northern Germany, Scandinavia, and some parts of Switzerland. The medieval Inquisition had its greatest effect in northern Italy and southern France. In the 1490's it began to spread into Spain. Geography thereby exerted an important influence on the development of opposition to religious domination by the Roman church. The modest expressions of theological diversity in Christendom prior to 1500 came from lands more geographically removed from the punitive arm of the Vatican.

In spite of the harsh suppressive measures of the medieval church, some differences of religious opinion did appear in several places by the end of the Middle Ages. There was little sense of religious tolerance as we understand it today, but there was some expression of religious diversity.

The mystics within the ranks of the church, such as Catherine of Siena, emphasized a personal piety and a direct relationship between God and man with no intermediary such as the church. Humanists both inside and outside the church stressed the importance of man's well-being in this present earthly life. They opposed a basic idea of medieval Christianity that man's life in this world is important only as it shapes his soul and God's mercy in the next life.

Humanist views were strongly articulated by Erasmus (1466 – 1536), the Dutch satirist, who remained within the ranks of the church as its prestige and power began to wane. Yet this eminent writer of the northern Renaissance contributed much to the growing opposition toward Rome. He aided the effort seeking more openness in Christian thought and doctrine. Some observers have commented that Erasmus laid the egg of protest against the papacy that was later hatched by Martin Luther.

The culture of England during this period was deeply affected by anticlericalism and the movement toward a modicum of religious tolerance. English nationalism became increasingly intermixed with a long tradition of opposition to the clerical power centered in Rome. In the middle of the twelfth century Henry II had sought to extend royal authority over the church in England by requiring the clergy to swear fealty to the king and submit to justice in royal courts rather than in ecclesiastical courts. These reforms were hampered for a time by the hostile popular reaction when Thomas Becket, the Archbishop of Canterbury, was assassinated by some of Henry's overzealous subordinates.

Yet divisions within the leadership of the church in Rome aided the dissidence promoted by John Wycliffe and the Lollards operating from Oxford University. The English theologian William of Ockham voiced bitter denunciations toward the absolutism of the papacy. English literature expressed a unique form of anticlericalism through the vigor and pride of a new national language. William Langland and Geoffrey

Chaucer from somewhat different perspectives wrote masterpieces of poetry containing pungent messages against the authority of the church.
Hollister wrote about these two early English critics of medieval society
as follows:

> The works of these two men mark the emergence of
> the English language as a dominant literary vehicle
> after centuries of French linguistic supremacy. And
> both men disclose — each in his own manner — the
> growing popular hostility toward the ecclesiastical
> establishment. [10]

Beyond the Middle Ages

The explanation of three conditions for a religious and social environment favorable to the restoration of Christian healing by the end of the
Middle Ages has been presented in what I consider to be the order of
their levels of development.

Public access to the Bible was at the highest level of development.
Thousands of copies printed in national languages were being read and
distributed both openly and clandestinely. Within a few decades the religious and political effect of increasing exposure to the Bible was enormous. Western and Central Europe were never again the same. Public
reading of the Bible played a decisive role in the Protestant Reformation
and in the formation of sizable organized religious movements separated
from the Roman church. The Bible quickly became the primary source
of values fostering individual and national freedom.

The institutionalization of individual freedom emerged much more
slowly in the governmental structures and system of law in England. It
did not yet promote freedom of thought and action sufficient for the
imaginative and persistent effort required for establishing Christian healing. Several centuries would be needed before a suitable mental climate
could be developed for higher levels of religious freedom, including the
freedom to practice spiritual healing. This kind of environment was first
reached, not in England, but in the United States. The institutionalization
of individual freedom in America was built largely on English values,
but it assumed a somewhat different form than in its "mother country."

The requirement for a culture embracing religious tolerance was the
least developed of the three conditions at the end of the Middle Ages. Intense religious intolerance on the continent soon erupted in bitter and destructive warfare that lasted on and off for another several centuries.

Genuine religious tolerance suitable for the growth of Christian healing did not appear in countries such as Germany, France, Italy, and Spain until the twentieth century.

Religious tolerance advanced gradually in England after the "Glorious Revolution" in the seventeenth century and the passage of an Act of Toleration by Parliament in 1689. By this time England had several Christian denominations. Yet in spite of this statutory law, considerable religious intolerance continued in some areas of English society.

Religious tolerance grew in a somewhat different form in the United States, where the Constitution included a Bill of Rights upholding the freedom of religion and the separation of church and state. In a relatively short period of time, America became a land of numerous Christian churches and widespread religious pluralism. As in England, religious intolerance persisted in various classes and regions of this large country.

The social environment in some Western societies after 1500 has been enhanced by inspired and courageous Christian thinkers performing important works of healing. These persons have served as planters of the seed needed to germinate in good soil and bring spiritual healing back into the Christian church.They have helped in spreading stronger and deeper roots for the growth of this neglected legacy of early Christianity.

At first this planting was modest and intermittent. Near the end of his life Martin Luther healed his co-worker, Philip Melanchthon, of a serious illness through faith and prayer. In the mid-seventeenth century George Fox founded the Quakers or Society of Friends and performed numerous healings by spiritual means in England and the American colonies. In the eighteenth century John Wesley established the Methodist Church in England and also healed in his own country as well as in the American colonies.

Spiritual healing, however, did not become an integral part of the teachings and practice of any Christian church until the nineteenth and twentieth centuries. This move occurred in both America and England. From these two pillars of English-speaking culture, Christian healing has gradually spread to other parts of the world. This restoration has been guided by reliance on the Bible as the source of inspiration and instruction in healing the sick and in reestablishing the healing mission of the early Christian church.

This achievement was begun by the formation of the Christian Science church by Mary Baker Eddy in the 1860's and 1870's in Boston, Massachusetts. According to its Manual, the basic purpose of the Church of Christ, Scientist, is "to organize a church designed to commemorate the word and works of our Master, which should reinstate primitive Christianity and its lost element of healing."[11] The founding of the Christian Science church influenced the beginning of other religious organizations seeking to heal disease by spiritual means. These churches and groups included the Unity School of Christianity, the Emmanuel Movement, and the Church of Religious Science.

The Pentecostal-Charismatic movement led by A. J. Tomlinson and Charles G. Parham began to spread in several areas in the United States after the 1890's. This religious revival derived much of its underlying purpose from the account of the Day of Pentecost in the second chapter of the book of Acts. Pentecostals believed strongly in baptism and the gifts of the Spirit, one of which was speaking in tongues. As they performed this New Testament custom in their religious services, they discovered a second gift — the gift of healing. A historian of this religious movement wrote:

> In addition to the baptism of the Holy Ghost, pentecostals believed that nine Biblical gifts of the Spirit —
> the word of wisdom, the word of knowledge, the gift
> of faith, the gift of healing, the gift of miracles, the gift
> of prophecy, the gift of discerning spirits, the gift of
> tongues, and the gift of interpretation of tongues —
> were available to Christians today.[12]

The pentecostal emphasis on gifts of the Spirit, including the gift of healing, has spread to other Christian denominations.

Christian healing has emerged in large mainline churches during the twentieth century from the efforts of numerous devoted clergymen and lay women. These persons include Percy Dearmer, Leslie Weatherhead, Evelyn Frost, Agnes Sanford, Morton Kelsey, Francis MacNutt, Emily Gardner Neal, and Barbara Shlemon. Interdenominational movements dedicated to the mission of Christian healing have also exerted a large impact. Two contemporary organizations are the International Order of St. Luke The Physician, established in 1935 by Reverend John Gayner Banks; and the Institute for Christian Renewal, organized in 1980 by Reverend Mark Pearson. This widespread mission in many Christian churches is also based on the healing message of the Bible. One of its articulate spokesmen declared:

> Healing is at the very heart of who God is. The Bible
> tells us repeatedly that God is all-powerful and all-loving. These words remain platitudes — and God re-

mains an abstraction — until they are applied in real situations. To say that God is love and yet not see Him at work in people's lives is a cruel contradiction. The God we worship is not an absentee landlord, but a loving, caring Father who ministers to His children at their points of need. Sometimes the need is for healing. [13]

The work of these and many other Christians on behalf of the cause of reestablishing spiritual healing in the Christian church constitutes a fascinating and encouraging chapter in the history of Christianity. It is a chapter containing many accomplishments and victories. It is also a chapter with many trials and challenges.

Yet a detailed explanation of this important restoration in the evolution of Western civilization and our contemporary world is the subject matter of another book.

NOTES

PART ONE

1. Exodus 3 & 4.
2. I Kings 17.
3. II Kings 4 & 5.
4. Marchette Chute, *The Search for God,* (New Jersey, 1969), pp. 15–6.
5. Job 42: 10.
6. Genesis 1: 26.
7. Proverbs 3: 1, 2, 7 , 8.
8. Isaiah 51: 11, 12.
9. Isaiah 61: 1, 2.
10. Matthew 4: 23. Italics added.
11. D. Scott Rogo, "Spiritual Healing and the Christian Tradition: An Interview with Morton T. Kelsey," *Science of Mind*, (May 1989), pp. 12–13.
12. Matthew 5: 48.
13. John 8: 32.
14. Acts 9: 36–42.
15. Acts 28: 1–9.
16. Arnobius, *Against the Heathen,* 49.
17. *Ibid,* 50.
18. Daniel 3: 16–8.
19. Luke 13: 15–7.
20. Tertullian, *To Scapula,* Chap. IV.
21. Abba Eban, *Heritage: Civilization and the Jews* (New York, 1984), p. 58.
22. John 14: 12.
23. John 9: 4.
24. Colossians 2: 8.
25. Reverend Canon Mark A. Pearson, "Common Questions and their not-so common answers about the ministry of Christian healing," *Sharing (*April 1990), p. 14.
26. For a scholarly explanation of the healing mission in the Eastern Orthodox Church see Stanley Samuel Harakas, *Health and Medicine in the Eastern Orthodox Tradition (*New York, 1990), Chaps. I–III.
27. See Wayne A. Meeks, *The First Urban Christians: The Social World of the Apostle Paul* (New Haven, 1983), Chaps. 1, 2.
28. Donald Kagan, Steven Ozment, and Frank M. Turner, *The Western Heritage to 1715* (New York, 1987), p. 199.
29. Peter Brown, *The World of Late Antiquity A.D. 150–750 (*New York, 1971), pp. 189–203.

30. W.H.C. Frend, *The Early Church* (Philadelphia, 1982), p. 75.
31. Will Durant, *The Age of Faith* (New York, 1950), p. 767.
32. John 18: 36.
33. Elaine Pagels, *Adam, Eve, and the Serpent* (New York, 1988), p. 81.
34. Matthew 22: 21.
35. Tertullian, *Apology*, 39.
36. Pagels, p. 150.
37. Williston Walker, et. al., *A History of the Christian Church* (New York, 1985), Chap. 7.
38. See Thomas Bokenkotter, *A Concise History of the Catholic Church* (New York, 1979), pp. 136–42.
39. Morton T. Kelsey, *Psychology, Medicine, and Christian Healing* (San Francisco), 1988, p. 154.
40. *Ibid*, p. 155.
41. John 9: 3.
42. Walker, et. al. pp. 283–284.
43. Bokenkotter, p. 165.
44. Walker, et. al. pp. 288–289.
45. Kagan, et. al., pp. 245–254.
46. Bokenkotter, p. 166.
47. Mark 5: 25–34; Luke 8: 43–8.
48. Acts 5: 12–6.
49. John 4: 46–53.
50. Matthew 8: 5–13; Luke 7: 2–10.
51. Peters, pp. 196–9.
52. Walker, et. al.,pp. 332–48.
53. Durant, p. 930.
54. Bokenkotter, p. 171.
55. Kelsey, pp. 165–6.
56. Luke 8: 43–44.
57. James 5: 14, 15.
58. Tatian, *Address of Tatian to the Greeks*, Chap. XVIII.
59. Jack W. Provonsha, M.D., "The Healing Christ," *Current Medical Digest* (December 1959).
60. Durant, pp. 1003–1005.
61. Peters, pp. 270–271.
62. Barbara W. Tuchman, *A Distant Mirror: The Calamitous 14th Century* (New York, 1978), p. 95.
63. Winston S. Churchill, *A History of the English Speaking Peoples*, Volume 1, (New York, 1956), p. 353.
64. Tuchman, p. 104.
65. *Ibid*., p. 124.
66. Joan Evans, Editor. *The Flowering of the Middle Ages*, Thames and Hudson (London, 1966), p. 333.
67. See pp. 29–33.
68. James 5: 14, 15.
69. See Barbara Leahy Shlemon, Dennis Linn, and Matthew Linn, *To Heal as Jesus Healed* (Notre Dame, Indiana, 1986), pp. 21–23.
70. Francis MacNutt, *Healing* (Notre Dame, Indiana, 1985), pp. 69–70.

71. Luke 5: 23.
72. John 10: 10; John 5: 39.
73. Matthew 23: 23.
74. Tony Lane, *Harper's Concise Book of Christian Faith* (San Francisco, 1984), p. 40.
75. Henry Chadwick, *Augustine*, New York, 1986, p. 3.
76. Robert Payne, *The Fathers of the Western Church* (New York, 1989), Chap. VI.
77. *The Interpreter's Dictionary of the Bible* (Nashville, Tennessee, 1986), p. 371.
78. Romans 8: 1, 2.
79. Pagels, p. 150.
80. Titus 2: 11.
81. Bokenkotter, p. 172.
82. Durant, p. 949.
83. G. K. Chesterton, *Saint Thomas Aquinas* (New York, 1956), p. 31.
84. Walker, p. 333.
85. Durant, p. 955.
86. Chesterton, p. 71.
87. Bokenkotter, p. 168.
88. Chesterton, p. 32–3.
89. Quoted in Kelsey, p. 172.
90. *Ibid.*
91. Durant, p.54.
92. Kelsey, p. 152.
93. Mac Nutt, p. 280.
94. Walker, pp. 308–10.
95. Laura H. Wild, "English Translations of the Bible," in *The Abingdon Bible Commentary*, Abingdon-Cokesbury Press, Inc. (New York, 1929), p. 81.
96. Walker, p. 380.
97. Wild, p. 82.
98. *Ibid.*
99. Walker, p. 382.
100. Wild, p. 82.
101. Revelations 1: 6.

PART TWO

CHAPTER 1 ATHANASIUS

1. Robert Payne, *The Fathers of the Eastern Church* (New York, 1989), p. 68.
2. Ernest Leigh-Bennett, *Handbook of the Early Christian Fathers* (London, 1920), p. 152.
3. Payne, p. 67.
4. *Ibid.,* p. 68.
5. Hans von Campenhausen, *The Fathers of the Greek Church* (New York, 1959), p. 68.
6. E. G. Weltin, *Athens and Jerusalem: An Interpretative Essay on Christianity and Classical Culture* (Atlanta, Georgia, 1987), p. 92.

7. *Ibid.*, p. 54.
8. Payne, p. 73.
9. Campenhausen, p. 78.
10. Payne, p. 105.

CHAPTER 2 JEROME

1. Durant, p. 51.
2. Bokenkotter, p. 74.
3. Payne, p. 88.
4. Kelsey, p. 151.

CHAPTER 3 AUGUSTINE

1. Kelsey, p. 145.
2. Weltin, p. 111.

CHAPTER 4 SULPICIUS SEVERUS

1. Kelsey, p. 149.
2. Bernard M. Peebles, "Introduction to the Writings of Sulpicius Severus", in
   Roy Joseph Deferrari (ed.), *The Fathers of the Church* (New York, 1949).,
   p. 79.

CHAPTER 5 HEALERS IN THE
EASTERN ORTHODOX CHURCH

1. Walker, pp. 176 – 180.
2. Ibid., pp.142 – 144.
3. Darrel W. Amundsen, "Medicine and Faith in Early Christianity," *Bulletin of
   the History of Medicine*, (1982), p.341.
4. Stanley Samuel Harakas, *Health and Medicine in the Eastern Orthodox Tradition* (New York, 1990), pp. 72 – 75.
5. Quoted in Stanley Samuel Harakas, "The Eastern Orthodox Tradition," in
   Caring and Curing: Health and Medicine in the Western Religious Traditions
   (New York, 1986), p. 154.
6. Harakas, *Health and Medicine*, p. 73.
7. Ibid., p. 106.
8. Robert Payne, *The Fathers of the Eastern Church* (New York, 1985), p. 194.
9. Ibid., p. 168.

CHAPTER 6 CUTHBERT AND BEDE

1. Walker, pp. 224 – 225.
2. Benedicta Ward, *Miracles and the Medieval Mind* (Philadelphia, 1982), pp. 56 – 62.
3. Bertram Colgrave, "Introduction," *Two Lives of Saint Cuthbert* (New York, 1940), p. 10.
4. Durant, p. 488.
5. Ward, p. 58.
6. Leo Sherley-Price, "Introduction," *Bede: A History of the English Church and People* (New York, 1968), p. 29.
7. *Ibid.*, pp. 30 – 31.

CHAPTER 7 BERNARD OF CLAIRVAUX AND MALACHY

1. Bokenkotter, pp. 157 – 158.
2. Durant, p. 791.
3. Walker, p. 295.
4. M. Theodore Ratisbonne, *Histoire de S. Bernard*, Paris, (1843), quoted in Percy Dearmer, *Body and Soul* (New York, 1909), p. 359.
5. J. Cotter Morison, *Life and Times of St. Bernard*, (1868), quoted in Dearmer, p. 359.
6. Ibid., p. 360.
7. Bruno S. James, *Saint Bernard of Clairvaux: An Essay in Biography* (New York, 1957), p. 39.
8. Ibid., pp. 39 – 40.
9. Ward, p. 175.
10. Quoted in Ibid., p. 180.

CHAPTER 8 FRANCIS OF ASSISI

1. Pelikan, p. 133.
2. Dearmer, p. 361.
3. Pelikan, p. 134.
4. Durant, p. 793.
5. Pelikan, p. 136.
6. Durant, p. 801.
7. Pelikan, p. 140.
8. C. Warren Hollister, *The Making of England* (Lexington, Massachusetts, 1988), p. 263.

CHAPTER 9 CATHERINE OF SIENA

1. Walker, p. 359.
2. J. M. Perrin, *Catherine of Siena,* (Westminster, Maryland, 1965), p. 111.
3. Edith Deen, *Great Women of the Christian Faith* (New York, 1959), p. 52.
4. *Ibid.,* p. 58.

PART THREE

1. Evelyn Frost, *Christian Healing* (London, 1940), pp. 7 – 8.
2. Wild, pp. 80 – 87.
3. F.F. Bruce, *The English Bible: A History of Translation*s (New York, 1961), pp. 12 – 13.
4. Wild, p. 8.
5. Lacey B. Smith, *This Realm of England* (Lexington, Massachusetts, 1988), p. 79.
6. Hollister, p. 127.
7. Churchill, p. 253.
8. Smith, p. 96.
9. Durant, p. 784.
10. Hollister, p. 292.
11. *Church Manual of the First Church of Christ, Scientist, in Boston, Massachusetts,* Mary Baker Eddy, p. 17.
12. David Edwin Harrell, Jr., *All Things Are Possible: The Healing and Charismatic Revivals in Modern America* (Bloomington, Indiana, 1975), p. 12.
13. Mark A. Pearson, *Christian Healing: A Practical, Comprehensive Guide* (Old Tappan, New Jersey, 1990), p. 13.

INDEX

Additional copies of this book are available at

VISTA PUBLICATIONS
P. O. BOX 302
BOULDER, COLORADO 80306
The price is $13.95 postpaid.

Also available is the first study in a
series on the evolution of spiritual healing
based on the Bible.

This book is titled
Biblical Healing:
Hebrew and Christian Roots,
by Frank C. Darling.
The price is $10.95 postpaid.